ISLAND

GORDON KORMAN

BOOK THREE: ESCAPE

ISLAND

SCHOLASTIC INC.
New York Toronto London Auckland Sydney
Mexico City New Delhi Hong Kong Buenos Aires

ISBN-13: 978-0-439-16452-8
ISBN-10: 0-439-16452-4

Copyright © 2001 by Gordon Korman.
All rights reserved. Published by Scholastic Inc.
SCHOLASTIC, APPLE PAPERBACKS, and associated logos
are trademarks and/or registered trademarks of Scholastic Inc.

38 37 36   14 15 16/0

Printed in the U.S.A.   40

First Scholastic printing, August 2001

For Nicholas Parcharidis Jr.

SEPTEMBER 3, 1945
0835 hours

The Second World War ended on September 2, 1945, after the United States dropped two atomic bombs on Japanese cities. Most of the planet had suffered six terrible years of fighting and destruction, so there was rejoicing throughout the globe. Millions of soldiers worked around the clock to shut down their military operations and return to their families.

At a small U.S. Army Air Corps installation located on a tiny unnamed island in the Pacific, twenty-six airmen rushed to load equipment onto a transport plane bound for home. Their presence there had been so top secret that not even the Secretary of Defense knew about them. Their mission was to deploy a third atomic weapon — code name: Junior — a backup bomb. It was only to be dropped in the event that the first two failed to end the war.

The day was burning hot like every day on the tropical island. But today the sweat on the faces and bodies smelled distinctly of champagne. The celebration that marked the end of the war had set corks popping long into the

ESCAPE

night. Most of the men struggled through splitting headaches after little or no sleep.

When the heavy crane seized up, Staff Sergeant Raymond Holliday pounded the controls in frustration. "Blast these hydraulics!" The lift mechanism had been acting up for months, but it was impossible to get parts way out here in the Pacific. The crew had been told to "make do."

Barely a foot off the ground dangled Junior, the third bomb. Holliday tried the stick again. Nothing.

From the pit, Corporal Connerly hoisted himself up by the chain, setting his feet down on the curved surface of the bomb. He had no fear of the weapon going off. It would have to be armed first. "Dead?" he called to the sergeant.

Holliday scratched the fire-ant bites on his arms and thought longingly of his home in Michigan. "For good this time."

Both men looked to the landing strip a quarter of a mile away. Junior weighed over nine thousand pounds. Without the crane, there was no way to get it into the plane's cargo bay. They were silent as the sun beat down.

"We're going to be the last guys home from this war," Connerly said with melancholy conviction. "And for what? To nursemaid a souped-up firecracker on an island that Rand McNally him-self couldn't find with a telescope!"

The corporal was wrong on two counts. First, he was reunited with his family within forty-eight hours. And second, someone did find the tiny se-cret island.

Fifty-six years later, six young people, sur-vivors of a deadly shipwreck, washed up on the sandy shores.

ESCAPE

CHAPTER ONE
Day 16, 3:35 P.M.

Luke Haggerty peered out between the palm fronds. "Call me crazy," he said in amazement, "but I think that's a *chicken*."

The feathered creature perched on a fallen log was smaller than a farm hen, and a deep rusty brown rather than the usual white, speckled, or Rhode Island red. Otherwise, it was a dead ringer — the same four-toed bird feet, fleshy crest, and gizzard. It bobbed as it moved, pecking absently at the rotted wood, clucking softly.

"It *is* a chicken," confirmed his companion, Ian Sikorsky. "Before they were bred for food thousands of years ago, all chickens were like this — the Pacific jungle fowl, living in the wild."

Luke shot him a cockeyed look. "You're putting me on."

"No, really," Ian insisted. "It was in a show I saw on the Discovery Channel. This is a living fossil."

Luke grinned at the younger boy. He knew from experience that Ian was never wrong about something he'd seen on TV. Pushing up his too-long sleeves, Luke stepped out from behind the

ISLAND

tree. With their own shorts and T-shirts in rags, the castaways had taken to wearing fatigues from the abandoned army installation on the other side of the island. These were in perfect shape, if a little faded. But they were adult size. Slight Ian's new clothes hung on him like a tent.

Ian grabbed the baggy fabric of Luke's shirt. "Where are you going?"

"We've been living on fish and bananas," Luke replied. "If that's a chicken, it's dinner. It'll be our present for Will."

Will Greenfield rested back at their camp with a bullet wound in his thigh. Today was his birthday, or at least as nearly as they could reckon the date it was. There had been so little to celebrate lately — so much danger, so much fear. But real meat — their first in weeks — that would be a worthy present. It would also be the only present. As their fellow castaway J.J. Lane put it, "None of these coconut trees take American Express."

Luke approached the log from behind, stepping softly in the tangle of vines and underbrush. The bird clucked and pecked, seemingly unaware. Then, just as the boy lunged, it took off, flapping furiously. Luke tumbled painfully over the log, landing in a heap on the ground. Ian grabbed at the fowl, but it beat its wings in his face before flying off through the rain forest.

ESCAPE

Yelling, Luke ran after it, Ian hot on his heels. It was an awkward chase. Every ten feet or so, the bird would have to land, its chicken legs pumping like miniature pistons before it could take off again. The castaways were faster, but they had the jungle to contend with. Branches and palm fronds slashed at their bodies and faces, and low vines tripped them up.

Ian pointed. "It's heading for the beach!"

Lyssa Greenfield handed her brother, Will, a small aluminum cup of water and a single pill. "Happy birthday," she said dryly.

Will sat up on his "hospital bed," the wooden raft that had brought four of the castaways to the island more than two weeks earlier. "It's better than what you gave me last year — cracked ribs."

"You melted my computer disks," she reminded him.

Will swallowed the capsule and regarded his sister. She looked too upset to be still angry over a fight they'd had a year ago. "What's the matter, Lyss? Was that the last pill?"

Ever since the shooting, Will had been taking the antibiotics from the first-aid kit. He was pretty certain that this was what had kept infection from setting in. But he had always known that the pills would not last forever.

She nodded. "Great present, huh?"

Will tried to sound upbeat. "It doesn't hurt anymore. It's just kind of numb."

Lyssa tried to hide her wince. The patient always looked away when his bandage was being changed, but Lyssa had seen that wound — swollen black and blue around a tattered, gaping hole. Add infection to that —

Infection. At home or in a hospital, it was a pretty simple thing. But here in this sweltering, insect-laden humidity, with medical attention hundreds of miles away, it was a death sentence.

Her brother struggled up to his knees and tried to shift a little weight to his bad side. He shrugged. "With any luck it's healed already."

With any luck. Luck had abandoned them so long ago that Lyssa couldn't remember what it felt like to be lucky. Not just shipwrecked — *marooned* on an uncharted island. And then there were the smugglers — murderous dealers in ivory and illegal animal parts. They were gone now, flown off in their floatplanes. But they would be back. The old military installation was the perfect place for them to carry on their illicit trade.

Anyway, the damage had already been

done. The bullet in Will's leg had come from one of their guns. Not on purpose — the smugglers had no idea there was anyone else on the island. No, it had been a stray shot. Collateral damage. Yet another piece of the castaways' brand of luck.

She grimaced inwardly. There was also this little matter of an atomic bomb. Of course, it had been there for more than fifty years, so it probably wasn't going to go off in their faces. But if the smugglers ever found it . . .

She tried to smile over at Will, but the corners of her mouth simply refused to turn up. Small wonder. Lyssa honestly felt she might never smile again.

Suddenly, a cry from the jungle:

"Dinner! *Dinner!*"

The Greenfields exchanged a bewildered look. That was Ian. What was he babbling about?

As they watched, Luke and Ian burst out onto the beach. They were running full speed and screaming. What was Luke saying?

"Grab that chicken!"

Chicken?!

But then Lyssa saw it — a scrawny, under-sized brown hen, flap-hopping for its life.

"I got it!" Charla Swann ran across the beach, lining up the bird with her keen athlete's eye. She lunged, arms outstretched, hands ready. But the fowl squawked loudly and scrambled just out of her reach. Charla went down, eating sand.

The sixth castaway, J.J. Lane, pulled a four-foot branch out of the woodpile. "There's only one way to hit a knuckleball." He cocked it back over his shoulder and took a home-run swing.

"Strike one!" he cheered, fanning.

"Get out of the way!" panted Luke.

But J.J. lined up the chicken and took another cut. "Strike two!"

Will flattened himself to the raft. "Hey, watch it with that thing!"

But it was hard to stop J.J. once he had decided on a course of action. He raced into position, colliding with Luke, sending the two of them staggering. J.J. recovered, pulled back his "bat," and took his final swing. "Strike — "

Whack!

J.J. himself was the most surprised person on the beach when he made contact. The bird sailed twenty feet through the air and fell to the sand, stone dead. J.J. dropped the branch as if it had suddenly become electrified.

ESCAPE

Charla turned on him. "J.J. Lane, how could you do that to an innocent little bird?"

"And why were *you* chasing it?" J.J. sneered. "To give it a check from Publishers Clearing House?"

"No, this is good!" Ian exclaimed. "It's a Pacific jungle fowl — "

"It's Will's birthday present!" added Luke, glaring at J.J.

Charla was still mad. "You didn't have to bludgeon it!"

J.J.'s father was the movie star Jonathan Lane. Growing up in a rich and powerful family had given him little patience for criticism. "The bird had to die somehow, right?" he argued. "What difference does it make if I Babe-Ruthed it?"

"It makes a difference to the bird," Charla insisted.

"Not anymore," J.J. chuckled.

Luke turned his attention away from his irritation with J.J. "This is *meat*. Less fighting; more eating."

The castaways soon learned that having meat was much more complicated than merely opening a shrink-wrapped package from the supermarket. The fowl's head and feet had to be removed. The carcass had to be sliced open. It was a gruesome job. The smell of warm blood in the tropical humidity was nauseating. Luke fought hard to keep from throwing up as he used the knife from their survival pack to scoop the innards away. Lyssa held her nose with one hand while using the other to bury the mess in the sand.

"I don't think I can eat it now," breathed Charla.

"We've come this far," Luke groaned. Out of the corner of his eye, he caught sight of J.J. strolling away. "What do you think you're doing?"

The actor's son paused. "When the going gets tough, the tough get going. I thought I'd, you know, get going. Maybe take a swim — "

For Luke it was the last straw. J.J. was always goofing off. The spoiled Hollywood brat had probably never done any real work in his life and for sure not any dirty work. Daddy's staff took care of all that.

But the famous Jonathan Lane wasn't here right now.

Luke stood up. "All right, smart guy. You're going to pluck this chicken."

"In your dreams," laughed J.J. "If it wasn't for me, you'd still be chasing that dumb bird around the beach. I'm the hunter; you guys are the kitchen staff."

Luke fixed the actor's son with a murderous

look. "No matter what we do, you're always standing around cracking jokes. Well, today you're going to make yourself useful." He held out the bloody carcass.

"If you don't want that up your nose," J.J. said warningly, "get it out of my face."

"I'm not falling for that!" snarled Luke. "Fighting's just another way for you to goof off!"

"You and me," J.J. said evenly. "Right here, right now."

"*Enough!*"

It was a cry from Will that froze everyone like the subjects in a still picture.

"I don't want any chicken!" Will exclaimed bitterly. "Not if it means a big stink like this! It's my birthday, and I'm lost, and I'm shot up, and I'm probably never going to see another one! So take that dumb chicken and throw it in the ocean for the fish!"

J.J. snatched the carcass out of Luke's hand. "I'll pluck it," he mumbled.

"I can help," Ian volunteered.

"Forget it," said J.J. "Go watch the Discovery Channel."

CHAPTER TWO
Day 16, 5:05 P.M.

Blood and feathers. Ugh . . .

In no time, J.J. was covered in both. He'd never forgive the others for this!

Not fair for them to gang up on him. They were jealous — that was pretty plain. They were nobodies, especially Luke, a kid with a criminal record. He said he was innocent — that someone else had stashed that gun in his locker. But that was probably a lie. The kid was so full of himself. Look at how he pushed everybody around, acting like the leader of the castaways. Who voted him king?

Not me, that's for sure!

One stubborn tail feather wouldn't come out. J.J. yanked with both hands. As it jerked free, a splatter of blood hit him in the eye.

"Ow!"

Hard to believe — no, *impossible* — that barely a month ago, he'd been lounging around the pool with Gwyneth Paltrow and Julia Roberts. Then came the mistake. Okay, a few mistakes. Just a bunch of stuff to get his father's attention: a

ESCAPE

case of champagne at the eighth-grade dance, a couple of CDs at the five-finger discount, a ride on Dad's Harley through the front window of an art gallery on Rodeo Drive —

Yeah, he'd probably gone too far that time. It was what had earned him a ticket on Charting a New Course, a four-week boat trip for troubled youth. They had all done stupid things like that: Luke with the gun in his locker; Charla with her driven obsession to be a star athlete; Ian for being a TV-addicted couch potato; and Will and Lyssa for sibling warfare. Those were the offenses that had gotten them sent halfway around the world on a boat trip. Then — a few lousy breaks, and here they were.

A few lousy breaks. Yeah, right.

It was J.J.'s opinion that there had been no disaster. The wreck of the *Phoenix* and everything that had happened since was, he felt, all carefully planned by Charting a New Course. A trick boat, designed to "sink" — it was probably part submarine. By now it had resurfaced to be fixed up for the next group of suckers. Luke and the others said it was impossible. But they'd never lived in Hollywood, where special-effects wizards created the impossible every day.

So gullible! Wasn't it too much of a coincidence that two separate rafts had drifted to exactly the same tiny island? One that happened to be a rendezvous point for dangerous smugglers? It was a setup. The whole theme of CNC was learning teamwork and building character through adventure. J.J. was convinced the "smugglers" had been professional actors. The old military installation was fake too. Like the army would just *forget* an atomic bomb!

No one was in any danger. At the first sign of trouble, CNC would stop the simulation and send them all home. But the others insisted on playing Robinson Crusoe — living off the land, scrambling for coconuts and bananas. And now — gag! — a chicken.

J.J. could picture Captain Cascadden — who *supposedly* drowned — and Mr. Radford — who *supposedly* jumped ship and left them to die. For sure, the two men were watching the castaways on hidden cameras, high-fiving and laughing about how everything had unfolded exactly according to plan.

Well, *almost* according to plan. Will getting shot — that must have been a mistake. It was good news, really. At some point, Will needed to have that bullet removed from his leg. Which meant that any day now, CNC would stop this game and take the poor kid to a doctor. All the castaways had to do was wait it out.

ESCAPE

Blood spattered on J.J.'s shirt. He wheeled to face the jungle. That was where the hidden cameras probably were. "Hey, look!" he bellowed. "Jonathan Lane's only son is plucking a chicken! He's turning into a better person with every feather!"

The others were staring over at him, but nobody said a word. They thought he was nuts. J.J. knew better. Somewhere — in an office, or a plane, or a special surveillance boat — CNC was observing all this and making notes. He refused to give them the satisfaction of thinking that he couldn't see through their charade!

He stood up. "Hey, Haggerty."

When Luke looked over, J.J. tossed the plucked bird right to him in a chest pass.

"How do we cook it?" asked Lyssa.

Instantly, all eyes turned to Ian.

The younger boy backed up a step. "I don't know anything about cooking!"

"You spent your whole life in front of the TV," said J.J. "Didn't you ever catch Chef Emeril?"

Luke dismantled one of the three stills the castaways used to boil the salt out of seawater to make it drinkable. Using two sticks, he held the fowl over the fire, turning it like a rotating spit on a barbecue.

"Nothing's happening," Charla observed after a few breathless minutes.

So they tried cooking over the bonfire. This was a huge blaze — it was intended to alert passing planes and ships to their presence on the island. The sizzling sound was instant, along with a delicious smell of cooking meat. A split second later, half the bird was ablaze.

Lyssa beat at the fire with a plastic rain poncho, but that only fanned the flames, which spread to the sticks in Luke's hands.

Luke looked around in alarm. "Quick! Grab the chicken!"

"Are you crazy?" exclaimed Charla. "It's on fire!"

Lyssa held up the pot of freshwater from the dismantled still. Luke deposited the bird inside and dropped the burning sticks to the sand. A plop and a hiss, and Will's birthday dinner was extinguished.

Luke blew on his hands. "Thanks," he told Lyssa.

"Hey, why don't we just boil it?" suggested Charla. "You can boil anything, right?"

Lyssa hung the pot by its half-hoop handle over the fire. Since the water had just been boiling, it began to churn and bubble almost right away.

ESCAPE

"How long do we cook it for?" asked Will.

"Better make it a while," put in Charla. "Nothing is grosser than raw chicken."

Leaving the birthday dinner to boil, they went about their business. Ian's mission: find taro, a potatolike root vegetable that would make a good side dish. Luke went into the jungle with him, to collect firewood. Since large logs were rare, and smaller twigs and branches burned quickly, keeping the voracious bonfire going was a full-time job. Charla went along to help.

J.J. opted for a swim to wash away the blood, sweat, and feathers of his plucking experience. Only Lyssa stuck around to keep Will company. But there was work to do there too. She had to tend the bonfire and also the smaller fires on the two working stills. From these, she collected the bowls of freshwater and poured them into their keg. It, like most of their conveniences, came from the *Phoenix's* rubber lifeboat. Lyssa and J.J. had drifted to the island on this inflatable craft. Seven days lost at sea. The memory of it still brought her chills. But it had been a luxury cruise compared with what the other four had suffered — bobbing around on a tiny piece of the destroyed *Phoenix*, big enough only for three, while the fourth hung over the side. It was amazing any of them had survived — especially her brother, who was a suburban kid and kind of soft.

Sharply, she reminded herself that Will wasn't out of the woods yet. None of them were if they couldn't find a way off this island.

Now the covered lifeboat sat just inside the trees, where it served as the castaways' sleeping quarters.

Lyssa recorked the water keg and plucked three large snails from the sun canopy. These would go into the boiling pot as soon as the chicken was done.

The chicken. The position of the sun told her that more than an hour had passed. Surely the birthday dinner was ready by now.

She ran over and checked the pot. "Oh, no!" she gasped.

Will sat bolt upright on the raft. "Don't tell me you've burned my chicken!"

"No," she managed. "Not burned." How would you describe it? Pieces of meat and skin floated everywhere. Down in the bottom of the pot rested a small pile of bare bones. They had cooked the living daylights out of that poor little hen.

Painstakingly, she began spooning pieces of meat onto a plate. "They're going to kill me," she told Will.

"*I'm* going to kill you," Will retorted. "Is it ruined?"

"Not exactly. But it's not good either."

She was about to pour out the water when Will suddenly sniffed the air. "Lyss, I may be delirious, but — I think I smell Grandma's matzoh ball soup!"

Lyssa took a whiff, and then a taste of the water she had been about to dump. "It *is* soup!" she exclaimed in amazement. "We made chicken soup!"

Bouncing on his bottom, Will managed to "sit" his way over to the fire. He accepted a taste from his sister.

"Unbelievable!" he exclaimed. "We don't even have toilet paper, but we managed to cook homemade chicken soup! The others are going to drop dead!"

As Lyssa took another taste, she caught sight of her reflection in the aluminum pot.

The girl who thought she would never smile again was already smiling.

CHAPTER THREE
Day 17, 2:15 P.M.

Will ran a fever the very next day.

J.J. was the first to notice the flush in his face. "Dude, it looks like you're wearing old-lady makeup. Your cheeks are bright red."

For most of the afternoon, Will had been asking if the weather was getting colder. This close to the equator, the weather never got any colder, and the humidity stayed permanently at sweat-bath level.

"Chills," was Ian's diagnosis.

The thermometer in the first-aid kit confirmed that, yes, the patient was running a temperature of 99.8 degrees.

Will tried to treat it lightly. "Impossible," he wisecracked. "A person can't get sick after eating Grandma's chicken soup."

Lyssa took Luke and Ian aside. "That's not a high fever. It's okay, right?"

If she was looking to them for reassurance, she didn't get it.

"He's only been off the antibiotic for a day," Ian said nervously. "If there's an infection already, it could spread very fast."

Lyssa swore them both to secrecy. "I don't want Will worrying about this. He's such a wimp that he could make himself even sicker."

Luke looked thoughtful. "Maybe he was like that in his old life. But your brother's been through a lot in these last few weeks. He's not a pushover anymore."

But she was adamant. "Let's not play with his head — at least not until we know we've got trouble."

If they were fooling Will, they certainly weren't fooling Charla. "We should go back to the army base," she urged quietly. "They had alcohol and bandages. Maybe they've got some pills or something."

It was decided that Luke and Charla would go over to the other side of the island and raid the dispensary.

This was a trip the castaways didn't make very often, although it was less than two miles. The foliage was so dense, the vines and underbrush so tangled, the insects so relentless, that it wasn't a very pleasant walk. Even under the best of circumstances it took an hour and a half, but it could easily be double that. Since there was no trail, every journey was different, climbing over new-fallen logs, squeezing through new stands of ferns, ducking under new low-growing branches.

Luke hated these island crossings, and it wasn't just because of the mosquito bites. If the smugglers returned to their meeting place at the old base, there couldn't be any clue that there were others on the island. The slightest sign — a misplaced footprint, a fallen button — could alert these dangerous criminals to the castaways' presence. Luke had already seen them execute one of their own men without mercy. They would not hesitate to kill six kids to protect their illegal operation.

There was such a sameness to the rain forest that Luke and Charla clung to the few landmarks they knew. First came the crumbling concrete. It had once been the air base's runway, but now it was overgrown with jungle. From there, they became more careful because they knew the bomb pit was near. Luke had always assumed that nuclear devices were stored in high-tech containers. But back in World War Two, the atomic bombs had been kept right out in the open, in shallow pits just like this one. They had it on the authority of Ian and the Discovery Channel that this was true of Fat Man and Little Boy, the weapons that had actually been used. Junior, the third bomb, had been so top secret that the history books said it had never been built. But it made perfect sense that Junior would be housed the same way.

ESCAPE

Luke and Charla grew quiet as they drew close. Of course, you couldn't set off an atomic bomb by talking too loud. But they still felt a certain fearful respect for the awesome power of the device and the terrible destruction and death that had been brought about by its two brothers.

They exchanged a knowing glance as they passed a little notch on the trunk of a palm tree. Luke himself had made that mark. It told them that the pit was here, hidden in what looked like an unbroken expanse of jungle floor. He'd been unwilling to risk more obvious marking. There could be no greater disaster than having the smugglers find Junior. These men made money from the blood of endangered animals. They would not think twice about selling an atomic bomb to the highest bidder.

Charla put it on a more basic level. "This place gives me the creeps."

"Amen," Luke agreed.

At this point, the jungle was so dense that progress came closer to wading than walking. They pushed through ferns and twining vines. It still amazed Luke that the building remained invisible until he was practically close enough to touch it. The foliage was so thick and overgrown that there was a leaf here, a frond there, to obscure every inch of a hundred-foot Quonset hut.

Feeling their way along the corrugated metal, they headed for the rear, where two smaller huts were located. One of these showed a faded sign: DISPENSARY.

The door was off its hinges. Luke shoved it open and they stepped inside.

CHAPTER FOUR
Day 17, 4:35 P.M.

Mangosteens.

Will Greenfield sat up on his raft, working with a knife to cut open a mountain of the plum-sized fruit.

Mangosteens! In the world of naming foods, who had come up with that one? It sounded like a partner in his father's law firm: Berkowitz, Greenfield, and Mangosteen.

They were good, though. Actually, they were delicious. But that was beside the point. Six lives were in danger. Important work had to be done for their very survival. And what was Will's job? A mangosteen fruit salad.

Just because he'd had the bad luck to get shot. And now this fever. 99.8 degrees, and everyone was treating him like he was on his deathbed.

He'd run higher fevers from a bad cold.

For an instant, a sense of foreboding replaced his irritation. His thigh didn't hurt exactly, and the numbness was gone now, so that was a good sign, wasn't it? But still it felt somehow — *wrong*. There was a strange rhythmic throbbing, almost like a second heartbeat down there. One minute

ISLAND

the leg would seem strong enough for him to get up and dance. The next, it would be so weak he wasn't sure it would even support him.

No way! It was all in his imagination. And no wonder, with Lyssa moping around, looking at him like he was dying. He was perfectly okay. He could be helping — *contributing*! Not cutting up some fruit with a name that sounded more like a pediatrician.

Dr. Mangosteen will see you now. . . .

He looked around the beach. Everyone was busy. Even J.J. was fishing. Lyssa was fiddling with the lifeboat's broken radio. If they got off this island, Lyssa was probably going to end up the hero somehow. It was just the way things went for her — Lyssa, the beautiful, talented, straight-A student. And her older brother, the awkward, freckled slug.

He could picture his sister on the front page of every newspaper. Even on TV:

"Lyssa, how did it feel when you fixed the radio and made a long-distance antenna out of a banana to call in the marines to save you?"

After a long interview, the cameras would turn to Will. "Weren't you shipwrecked too? What was your job on the island?"

What would he tell them? *Oh, I sat around and cut up mangosteens.*

ESCAPE

And the reporter's face would go suddenly blank. "Cut up *what?*"

That was the story of his life with Lyssa. Will never had a chance to succeed. What kind of contribution could you make by sitting on a beach staring off into space?

And then he saw the black speck move. It was just over the horizon and getting larger every second.

Forgetting his wound, he leaped to his feet and immediately crumpled back to the raft.

"Plane!" he bellowed. "*Plane!*"

On the surface, it looked like pandemonium. But in reality, it was a carefully planned and well-practiced drill. Lyssa and J.J. dropped everything and raced to fill pots with seawater. Ian ran for the tarpaulin in the jungle. It was made of four rain ponchos sewn together and filled with dead leaves. He grabbed it and hauled it over to the bonfire.

If those leaves were thrown on the blaze and then the water dumped on top, the result would be a column of thick gray smoke that would extend hundreds of yards into the sky — an SOS that would be seen for miles around.

It was a moment the castaways had played over in their minds dozens of times — their chance at rescue.

Will had never felt more helpless. This could mean his life — all their lives! And he couldn't even walk. He got on his hands and knees and crawled across the sand to the bonfire.

Don't blow it! he tried to will the others. *Do everything exactly right!*

Still, they hesitated. They did not dare signal until they knew for sure whom they were signaling to. If they sent up the smoke, and the plane turned out to be carrying the smugglers, they'd be giving away their presence on the island. And that would be fatal.

Lyssa peered through the binoculars that had come with the survival kit.

Will tugged at the legs of her fatigues. "Can you see it? It's rescuers, right?"

She shook her head. "They're still too far off."

"Let's just go for it," urged J.J. "Get this over with one way or the other."

"Don't you dare!" snapped Lyssa. "Maybe you've got a death wish, but the rest of us want to live to grow up."

"This is awful," said Ian. "I wish we could just *know*."

"Wait a minute." Lyssa squinted into the binoculars. "It's banking to the side . . . it's definitely a floatplane . . . oh, my God!"

"What?" squeaked Ian.

"It's them! The smugglers!"

"Are you sure?" Will asked breathlessly. "All planes look alike!"

His sister shook her head. "Single engine, with a fat cargo hold underneath. It's them, all right."

Her words triggered more frantic action. But if the last drill had been fueled by hopeful anticipation, this one was driven by disappointment and dread. The castaways, even Will, began throwing sand on the bonfire. Soon the flames were smothered to nothing, and not a trace, not so much as a whiff of smoke, remained.

Will held on to his sister's shoulders and began to hop toward the lifeboat under cover of the trees. J.J. was hot on their heels. Ian brought up the rear, brushing their footprints from the sand with a leafy branch.

All four looked up. Through the canopy of the rain forest, they watched the floatplane descend over the island. As it swept overhead, suddenly one of the doors burst open. A dark object fell out and plummeted to the jungle below.

The castaways ducked, even though the thing was nowhere near them. They stayed down, bracing for — what? An explosion?

"Was that a *bomb*?" hissed Will.

"How could it be?" scoffed Lyssa. "They don't even know we're here!"

J.J. was the first to get up. "We're such saps. The guy was probably having a Big Mac and he tossed the bag so he wouldn't have to mess up the air base."

All at once, Lyssa froze. "The air base!" she exclaimed. "That's where Luke and Charla are!"

Will frowned. "What are they doing way over there?"

"Looking for medicine," she replied. "For you."

CHAPTER FIVE
Day 17, 5:35 P.M.

Whack! Whack! Whack!

Luke hacked at the rusty padlock with a sharp rock. With every blow that fell, a cloud of dust and cobwebs swirled up around him, making him cough.

The dispensary was set up like a doctor's office, with a single desk and chair, cabinet, and examining table. Nothing else had been needed. This small installation had never been home to more than thirty people. These had been the crew, pilots, technicians, and officers required to do a single job — to deliver an atomic bomb to its target.

Whack!

In a shower of rust flakes, the lock smashed and fell to the floor, disappearing in the weeds and rotted planking.

Luke opened the cabinet. "Jackpot." On the shelves stood dozens of medicine bottles.

Charla grabbed a couple and examined the labels. She looked up, her face blank. "How do we know which of this stuff could help Will?"

Luke grabbed the pillow from the examining

table, dumped out the stuffing, and began tossing bottles into the case. "We'll take it all," he decided. "With any luck, the Discovery Channel did a show on medicines."

"Right." Charla joined him. "Let's hurry up and get out of here. We don't want to be stuck in the middle of the jungle in the dark."

Luke tossed in a box of tongue depressors. It was dumb, he knew. Will had a bullet in his leg; no one was going to ask him to say "ah." He paused over a tray of surgical instruments.

Charla read his mind. "God forbid!"

But they took the tray anyway. They took everything, even the medic's journal, yellowed and tattered around the edges.

"You never know what might come in handy," Luke explained.

Charla nodded grimly. She no longer argued with any statement that began, "You never know . . ."

They were halfway out the door when the shouting began — loud, furious, and too close for comfort. It was so unexpected that, for a second or two, they froze, right in the open.

Charla snapped out of it first. She dragged Luke back inside the dispensary and pulled the broken door shut. They dropped to their knees and peered through the mud-streaked window.

ESCAPE

It was the smugglers! While Luke and Charla had been working in the Quonset hut, they had missed the sound of the floatplane landing. And now they were trapped. . . .

The leader was a hugely fat man in a pale green silk suit and matching fedora. His nickname had come from J.J.: Mr. Big. He was fatter than ever and in a towering rage about something.

"I don't care if he had *five* aces up his sleeve! You don't start a fistfight in a moving plane!"

"I'll find it! I'll find it!" promised a gravelly voice with a British accent.

In an amazingly graceful move for such a huge man, Mr. Big wheeled. As he turned, he pulled a large handgun from his pocket and pistol-whipped his unfortunate associate.

The sound of the blow, metal against human flesh, was a sickening thud. Huddled inside the dispensary, both Luke and Charla flinched.

The victim went down, and a third man quickly stepped between him and his boss.

Mr. Big wasn't finished yet. "You'll find it," he agreed, "or the next thing you'll find will be a bullet in your head!"

"It's too late now, boss," reasoned the third man. "It'll be dark soon. We'll have to look for it in the morning. What can happen to it? There's nobody here but us."

In the gloom of the dispensary, Luke and Charla exchanged an agonized look. Neither of them dared speak until the voices of the three men faded.

"Where are they?" asked Charla in something much less than a whisper.

"Probably in the main building," breathed Luke. "Or maybe down by the beach, getting stuff from the plane. Either way, we can't risk leaving now."

She nodded. "But when?"

In the diminishing light, she felt rather than saw Luke's shrug.

Night fell quickly in the tropics. With the thick rain forest blocking even starlight, the darkness in the dispensary became total and suffocating. There was an isolation to it, Luke thought. He knew Charla was only a few inches away, but he could not see her at all. They wouldn't make it ten feet in the jungle in this blackness.

They were stuck here until morning — stuck here together, yet separated by a complete absence of light.

He felt her hand steal into his. Her fingers were cold as ice.

ESCAPE

CHAPTER SIX
Day 18, 5:50 A.M.

Fear.

Charla couldn't believe some of things she used to consider fear. Like the butterflies as she crouched in the blocks, waiting for the starter's gun in an important race.

Tension, sure. Doubts, always. But fear?

These last few weeks had taught her the true meaning of fear: losing the captain at sea, dangling like shark bait from a tiny raft, facing a lifetime marooned.

And now cowering in the pitch-black of the dispensary, hiding from certain death.

That was fear.

All through the terrible night, she revisited her old anxieties: that moment, still in midair after the dismount from the balance beam, not yet knowing if she could stick the landing.

Nerve-wracking? Of course. Gut-wrenching? Maybe. Fear? Not even close.

Even her ultimate old fear — the disappointment on her father's face as he held up the stopwatch: "Now that wasn't exactly a personal best,

ISLAND

was it?" — made her smile in the darkness. In this place, this situation, who cared about a few hundredths of a second?

Her whole life so far had consisted of training and striving for athletic perfection. And right now that seemed about as important as ice cubes in the Arctic. . . .

"Charla — wake up."

Luke knelt before her, one hand over her mouth, the other shaking her by the shoulder.

She looked out the smeared, cracked glass. It was still dark, with just the first few tendrils of dawn creeping across the sky.

"Let's get out into the trees," Luke whispered. "Then we can wait for the light and take off."

They invested precious seconds closing the rickety door, determined that the dispensary should look as if no one had been there for decades. Then they were crawling through tightly woven underbrush, praying that the screeching of the awakening birds was covering the rustle of their movements.

They were well away from the Quonset huts by sunup. They found the broken concrete of the old runway with a minimum of wandering. From there, they were able to point themselves in the direction of their own side of the island.

ESCAPE

Charla let out a mournful sigh. "Can you believe that they're back so soon? We almost walked out of the hut right in their faces!"

"I thought we'd have more time," Luke agreed, hefting the pillowcase over his shoulder. "Man, was our signal fire a bust or what? We didn't even see a plane or boat, much less get rescued!"

"Nobody's looking for us," Charla reminded him. "We're dead, remember?"

It was true. Mr. Radford, the *Phoenix*'s mate who had abandoned them, was safely back on dry land. The smugglers had left behind a *USA Today* with the whole story — Radford telling the world that the six kids in his charge had all died in the shipwreck.

"Great guy, that Rat-face," said Luke bitterly. "He has the same warm, fuzzy personality as the Green Blimp back there."

Charla shuddered visibly. "That was awful! I can still hear the sound it made when he hit that man! I wonder what they lost."

"It must have been something important," Luke said grimly. "Mr. Big wouldn't threaten to kill somebody just to scare him. He's really ready to shoot that guy."

They walked in silence for a few moments, listening to the rustling of the palms as a slight wind blew. Luke reached up to brush a bug from his cheek. But instead of an insect, he felt his hand close on a small piece of paper.

Litter? In the jungle?

He looked down and saw Benjamin Franklin staring back at him. This was a *hundred-dollar bill*! Wordlessly, he showed it to Charla.

"Money!" she breathed.

Then they saw it, lying in the underbrush, its lock sprung — a black suitcase. It gaped open, and out of it poured neat bundles of bills, all hundreds.

"Oh, wow!" Luke groaned. "Now we know what they lost, and why they're so upset about it."

Mesmerized, Charla dropped to her knees and ran her hands over the pile of money. "In my neighborhood," she whispered, "this could buy — my neighborhood!"

"There's got to be a couple of million at least." Luke nodded. "They're going to come after it, no question."

Charla looked stricken. "Yeah, but it's like finding a needle in a haystack! It was a total accident that we found it! They'll have to search the island fern by fern. They'll stumble on our camp twenty times before they ever track down this suitcase!"

ESCAPE

Luke crouched beside her and began stuffing bundles of bills back into the luggage. "That's exactly why we have to help them."

"Help them?" Her voice was shrill. "We're dead if they even find out we're here! How can we help them?"

"By making the suitcase easier to find," Luke explained. "We just have to put it somewhere they're bound to notice."

"We can't lean it up against the door of the Quonset hut," she pointed out. "They'll know something's fishy."

"I'm not that stupid," said Luke. "We'll just take it closer to their camp and leave it out in the open. The sooner they find it, the sooner they stop looking."

At the castaways' camp, the gloom had begun the previous nightfall and had settled into despair with every passing hour.

Two facts: One, the smugglers were back; and two, Luke and Charla had gone over to the military installation and had not returned.

Ian mulled over the information every which way, but a single word kept bubbling to the surface: *caught.* The smugglers had them, and that meant they were probably dead.

He choked on a lump in his throat. Or maybe they were alive, being interrogated about who they were and who was with them.

He felt a surge of pride. Luke was strong; he would never talk! But the feeling evaporated in a second as he recalled a TV documentary on interrogation methods. Luke would talk. Everybody talked. Which meant the smugglers could be coming for them right now.

The night had been terrible. Ian was pretty sure no one had slept, except maybe Will, whose temperature had gone over 101, and who mumbled through fevered dreams. Everybody was sure they should be doing something, but no one could decide what that might be. Though the castaways had no official leader, without Luke they would never agree on a course of action. Luke was the mortar that held them together. And it was beginning to look as if he would never be back.

"Haggerty can't be dead," J.J. assured everyone. "He's too mean to die. And Charla — who could catch her?"

But even he looked worried. And he hid right along with the rest of them when they heard a rustling in the foliage.

Crouched in the underbrush, Ian let his mind

run riot. Would the castaways be discovered? How long could they stay hidden? Could Will keep up?

And then a surprised voice asked, "Where'd everybody go?"

"Luke!" cried Will.

It was interesting, Ian reflected during the celebration that followed. Things were not good and getting worse. Yet the glory of little triumphs like this — welcoming two friends back from the brink of death — would surely rank among his greatest memories. You know — if he lived long enough to have memories.

As the castaways shared accounts of the last day and night, they were able to piece together what had happened. During a fistfight over a poker game, the door of the smugglers' plane had been accidentally knocked open, and a suitcase full of money had dropped out over the jungle. Soon a second group of smugglers would arrive, carrying a shipment of elephant tusks, rhino horns, and other illegal animal parts. They were the sellers; Mr. Big was the customer. He needed the lost money to pay for his goods.

"So we left it where they're bound to find it," Charla concluded. "It's in plain sight in just about the only clear spot over by the air base."

Lyssa was horrified. "You *helped* them?"

"We helped ourselves," Luke amended. "The last thing we need is those guys combing the island."

Charla shook her head in wonder. "You should have seen it. Millions of dollars just lying there. I swear I was tempted to roll in it."

"It's fake," scoffed J.J.

Charla shot him a resentful look. "Even poor people know what money looks like."

J.J. was disgusted. "CNC can't print up a batch of phony bills that look real?"

Luke groaned. "We all know what you think. Let us think what we think."

Later, Luke, Lyssa, and Ian went through the pillowcase and tried to take stock of the supplies from the dispensary.

Lyssa was dubious. "Is any of this stuff even good after all that time?"

"There's no way of knowing," Ian replied. "I don't see penicillin, which is what we really need. The rest — " He shook his head. "I have no idea what most of it is for."

"This might help." Luke fished in the case and came up with the medic's journal. "Maybe it says something about bullet wounds."

All day and half the night, Ian pored over the fifty-six-year-old diary of Captain Hap Skelly, M.D. He devoured the details of Sergeant Holliday's fire-ant bites, Colonel Dupont's gout, and Lieutenant Bosco's stomach flu, searching for the tiniest hint of anything that might help Will. He skipped lunch and dinner too, reading by flashlight when it got dark. He owed it to Will, sure. But there was another reason.

For weeks, Ian had watched no television, surfed no Internet, and read not a single word. In the anxiety and fear of these terrible weeks, it had never crossed his mind how much he missed *information*.

On the beach of a tiny island in the vast Pacific, Ian felt like Ian again.

CHAPTER SEVEN
Day 19, 9:45 A.M.

Feb. 17, 1945. Having trouble keeping supplies. Who to order from? As far as the army's concerned, we don't exist on this tiny island. Can't even send letters home. Mission is too top secret. Our families must think we've vanished off the face of the earth.

Penicillin ran out weeks ago. Have been using an infusion of bitter melon — a local plant that resembles a small cucumber with acne. Seems to control Holliday's infection. But am I turning into a witch doctor?

Will hated the idea from the start. "What's an infusion?"

"It's sort of like making tea out of something," Ian replied, handing him a steaming cup.

The patient was appalled. "You guys have been plotting against me! I've been minding my own business here, and you've been picking weird jungle plants so you can poison me!"

"Most medicines come from tropical vegeta-

ESCAPE

tion," Ian explained. "I saw it in a show about saving the rain forest."

"That World War Two doctor said it was safe," added Luke.

"Forget it. I won't drink it."

But he did drink it, largely due to his sister's threat to have it poured down his throat. The complaining was a filibuster. Will never seemed to run out of new ways to describe the taste of bitter-melon tea — skunk juice, crankcase oil, toxic waste, boiled sweat, and Sasquatch drool, to name a few.

It became so entertaining to listen to his graphic descriptions as the day wore on that they almost lost sight of a very serious reality: Will's fever was still rising.

"It's not working," Lyssa whispered nervously. "Isn't there anything else we can give him? How about that stuff from the dispensary?"

"Well, there is one thing," Ian ventured reluctantly. "Novocain."

"Novocain?" laughed J.J. "What are you going to do — drill his teeth?"

Ian flushed. "Today Novocain is mostly used by dentists. But it can actually freeze any part of the body for surgery."

"You mean surgery on *Will*?" Lyssa was shaken by the sudden realization of what the younger boy was leading up to. "Shoot his leg full of painkiller and try to cut the bullet out?" She turned blazing eyes on him. "Are you *crazy*? It's only a little fever! He's not that sick!"

"I agree," said Ian. "But if he *gets* that sick, the bullet has to come out."

"In a nice clean hospital!" Lyssa added, a shrill edge to her voice. "With a doctor who didn't learn his job by watching the Surgery Channel!"

"Nobody's cutting up anybody," soothed Luke. "Ian's just laying out our options."

"This isn't an option," insisted Lyssa. "Never, never, never!"

Ian's expression plainly told her that *never* might come sooner than she thought.

The second group of smugglers arrived the very next afternoon. Will choked on a mouthful of bitter-melon tea when he spotted the aircraft.

Lyssa put her hands on her hips. "Oh, come on. Don't be such a baby."

Will kept on gagging and pointing.

"Plane!" shouted J.J.

Luke peered through the binoculars. "Twin-engine floatplane," he reported in a subdued tone. "It's them, all right."

Lyssa's hope popped before her like a soap

ESCAPE

bubble. For a few seconds, this plane had carried rescuers and not a fresh set of problems. Oh, God, what if help *never* came? What would happen to Will?

Watching her brother was like observing somebody with a bad flu. But while flu built, peaked, and then went away, this was growing worse with every passing moment.

That evening, Will's fever went well over 102 degrees. His face was flushed, his eyes were sunken, and he seemed languid and hazy.

In the middle of the night, he woke up the castaways with loud shouting. When Lyssa finally managed to shake him out of his nightmare, he was annoyed with her.

"Come on, Lyss, I'm trying to get some sleep. I'm not feeling so great, you know."

The next night, he kept everyone up with hours of high-pitched giggling.

"Hey," muttered J.J., "lose the laugh track."

But the snickers and guffaws continued until almost dawn. At that point, Will fell silent, dozing on and off all day. At four o'clock, his fever topped 103.

"That's bad, right?" he asked feebly, "That can't be good."

"You're burning up," Ian admitted. "We're going to take you down to the water and cool you off."

Luke and Ian helped Will into the surf. He was really weak, but once in the ocean he seemed better, with a natural buoyancy that made him comfortable in the water.

Will winced from the pain in his thigh. "Man, that stings!"

"Salt water's good for the infection," Ian reminded him. They had been applying compresses to the wound at every bandage change.

With a chest-pounding Tarzan yell, J.J. leaped off the high rocks at the edge of the cove and hit the waves with a drenching splash.

What a flake, Luke thought in disgust. *We're trying to keep Will from boiling over, and all it means to J.J. is a beach party.* Not to mention that it was just plain nuts to make unnecessary noise when the smugglers were on the island. Okay, J.J. made it pretty plain that he believed the whole thing was a CNC hoax. But surely, somewhere in the back of his mind there had to be a sliver of doubt. . . .

It had become the castaways' habit to enter the ocean fully clothed, letting their fatigues wash on their bodies. Then they would undress in the water, throw everything on the rocks, and go for

ESCAPE

a swim. The tropical sun was so hot that even the thick GI clothes dried almost instantly.

Luke had just pulled off his shirt when Will disappeared. One second he was bobbing like a cork; the next he had sunk out of sight, leaving barely a ripple.

CHAPTER EIGHT
Day 22, 4:40 P.M.

J.J. got there first, slapping at the waves, hollering, *"Will!"*

Luke grabbed his arms. "Cut it out! I can't see anything!" He stuck his face under and forced his eyes open, ignoring the stinging of the salt.

There was Will, curled up peacefully as if he had suddenly decided to go to sleep on the ocean floor.

Luke grabbed him under the arms and yanked his head up to the air. J.J. and Ian were right there, and they hustled Will, coughing and spitting, onto the beach.

The girls were already pounding across the sand, Charla out front with Lyssa hot on her heels.

"I'm okay!" Will tried to call, only to come up choking again.

"What happened?" gasped Lyssa.

"I don't know," Will wheezed. "I was swimming, and then — " He shrugged. "Then I was here."

"You blacked out," Luke informed him.

"But I feel better," Will insisted weakly. "In the

ESCAPE

water, it was like I was waking up for the first time all day."

Lyssa squeezed his hand.

"I'm losing it, Lyss," he confessed fearfully. "Even I can tell, and I'm the one who's losing it."

Lyssa swallowed a lump in her throat. "Ian had an idea — "

J.J. stared at her. "*That* idea? The operation? A few days ago you almost strangled the kid for mentioning it!"

There were tears in her eyes. "Things weren't so bad then."

"I'm always the last to know everything," Will complained. "What are you talking about? What operation?"

Luke filled him in on Ian's idea of using Novocain and surgical instruments to remove the bullet.

Will was round-eyed. "And I'd get better?"

Ian shuffled uncomfortably. "It's very risky."

Will spoke once more. "Riskier than doing nothing?"

His voice was quiet, but the logic of his words resounded like a cannon shot. Yes, if they botched this operation, Will would probably die. But if they just left him . . .

"Wait a minute." J.J. looked from face to face.

"You're *serious*? You say *I'm* crazy, and you want to cut someone open?"

"But if there's no other choice — " Will began.

"There's the choice of *not doing it!*" the actor's son exclaimed hotly.

"We have to help Will," Charla insisted.

"Don't let them!" J.J. pleaded with Will. "They'll mess you up real bad, and by the time CNC gets here to rescue us, it'll be too late!"

"I don't want to hear it," Lyssa said scornfully. "Who does less around here than you, J.J. Lane? We break our backs, and you treat this like some kind of tropical vacation! And now, suddenly, you're so concerned about Will? What a crock!"

J.J. took a step back, shocked and hurt. All at once, he wheeled and ran up the beach. "Hey, you!" he shouted at the trees. "Whoever's out there! It's over! You've got to come get us!"

"Whoa!" Luke exclaimed angrily. "We're not alone on this rock, remember?"

But J.J. was pleading with the hidden cameras and microphones he was sure were all over the jungle. "Hurry! They're gonna cut him! They're gonna *cut* him!"

Charla started after him. "Stop it, J.J.! There are *killers* on this island!"

ESCAPE

With a furious look back at her, J.J. ran into the trees. Charla moved to pursue.

"Let him go," ordered Luke.

"But the smugglers — " she protested.

"They're too far away. They won't hear anything."

The group straggled back to their camp. Lyssa helped her brother resettle himself on the raft.

"Captain!" J.J.'s voice carried from the jungle. "Mr. Radford! Whoever you are!"

Lyssa was nervous. "He'll come back, right?"

Luke nodded absently. "He always does. Listen, we need to talk. I've got an idea. And to be honest, it's scaring the daylights out of me." He took a deep breath. "But if it works out, nobody's going to have to operate on anyone."

Silence fell. Luke had everybody's attention. Ian leaned forward eagerly.

Even as Luke spoke the words, a part of him hung back, detached, amazed that it had come to this. Five months ago he had trusted a "friend" with his locker combination. A random inspection, a thirty-two-caliber pistol in Luke's rolled-up backpack . . .

But it isn't mine!

If the principal, the police, or the judge had believed those four simple words, everything would have been different. Luke Haggerty wouldn't be standing here, about to suggest the unthinkable. A plan that was little better than suicide.

"The smugglers leave their cargo in the float-planes," he explained, laboring to keep his voice steady. "There's no way they'd ever see me if I stowed away in one of the crates. The next morning they'd fly me off the island without even knowing I was there. Then all I'd have to do is slip away from them at the other end and go to the police."

"*All you have to do?*" Charla was horrified. "Luke, you're one kid. They're three adults with guns. Plus who knows how many guys waiting at the place where the plane lands."

"Yeah, but they'll be looking for the shipment, not me," Luke argued. "I'll climb out of the crate while we're in the air. Maybe I can stay hidden until there's a chance to make a run for it."

"That's a big maybe," said Ian. "You're dead if they catch you."

"Don't you think I know that? But look, we've been on this island almost a month and we haven't seen so much as a lousy canoe paddling by. Face it, the air force picked this place because it's totally nowhere. It took more than fifty

ESCAPE

years for somebody else to show up here — the smugglers and us. How'd you like to wait that long to be rescued?"

A gloomy silence descended on the group. Luke knew he had them. "Yeah, it's dangerous. But if we're ready to operate on Will, we should try this first. It's exactly the same risk — one life. And if it pays off, we get *rescued*. Once I'm back in the world, I can contact the police or the coast guard or somebody."

"How will they find us?" asked Lyssa. "I mean, you know the island, but you can't pick it out of a whole ocean."

Ian spoke up. "I've got some papers from the base that give our latitude and longitude."

Charla frowned. "When would you stow away? We have no way of knowing when the smugglers plan to leave."

"That's our biggest problem," Luke agreed. "Actually, I can't figure out why they didn't fly off a couple of days ago. How long could it take to trade the cargo for the money and scram? Why would they stick around?"

Ian looked puzzled. "You don't think — "

Charla read his mind. "The suitcase! They still haven't found the money! And they won't leave without it!"

"That's impossible!" Luke protested. "We left it

right out in the open near their camp! We did everything but put up a neon sign!"

"The jungle's a funny place," said Ian. "Your eyes play tricks on you in there."

Will looked even paler than usual. "If they don't have their money, that means they're probably out looking for it. We're lucky they didn't stumble into our camp by mistake."

"We can't let that happen," said Lyssa with gritted teeth. "First thing in the morning, we'll move the suitcase somewhere so obvious a blind man couldn't miss it."

"In the jungle there's no such place," Luke said thoughtfully. "We've got to do it *right* this time — even if we have to shove that suitcase down Fatso's throat!"

ESCAPE

CHAPTER NINE
Day 22, 11:55 P.M.

Luke dozed in and out of uneasy dreams to the raspy metronome of Will's tortured breathing. He had never been much of a sleeper at times of stress.

This isn't stress, he reminded himself. *This is being scared out of your mind.*

He lay awake, staring at the sun canopy that covered them. Outside, their small fire cast a dim glow through the rubberized material.

The others were asleep, and all was quiet except — the snap of a twig seemed as loud as a gunshot. He sat bolt upright, instantly alert. He could make out a silhouette against the canopy. Someone was out there!

The smugglers! His mind raced as he wracked his brain for a way to wake his fellow castaways without alerting the intruder.

And then the head turned. In profile, Luke caught a glimpse of the outline of sleek sunglasses.

He relaxed. It was J.J., back at last.

Only a true Hollywood idiot would wear shades at night on a deserted island. J.J. adored

ISLAND

those dumb glasses. He hardly ever took them off. They were one-of-a-kind frames, custom-made for J.J.'s father by Paul Smith, the fashion designer. Luke had an image of the boy blundering through the rain forest in the pitch-black, walking into trees because he refused to remove those ridiculous shades.

Luke picked his way around his sleeping companions. He noted that Will's face glistened with perspiration. Night sweats again. And getting worse.

He stepped through the flap. "Hey," he greeted.

J.J. stared into the fire, his arms hugging his knees. He didn't look up.

Luke tried again. "You okay?"

"Fine," came the hoarse reply.

Luke could tell that the actor's son had not been far away. Anyone who spent nighttime hours in the heavy rain forest would come out eaten alive by mosquitoes. J.J. had only a few bug bites. Most likely he had retreated to the edge of the jungle at the first sign of darkness. There he had remained hidden, too embarrassed or too stubborn to rejoin the group.

J.J. flipped up his shades, and in the glow of the fire Luke could see he had been crying. "Did you do it? Did you cut him?"

ESCAPE

Luke shook his head and explained his stow-away plan. "We just have to get that suitcase into the smugglers' hands," he finished. "We could use your help tomorrow."

"Forget it," said J.J. "Somebody has to stay here to meet CNC."

For the first time, Luke felt no jealousy toward the actor's son. When he looked at J.J. now, all he saw was a scared boy clinging to a half-baked theory because the alternative was just too awful. Because bad things like that didn't happen to a movie star's kid.

"You know, CNC isn't coming," Luke said almost kindly.

J.J. flipped the shades back down, shutting Luke out.

They had all messed up to get sent on the trip, Luke reflected. But in a strange way, J.J. was the grand champion mess of the group. For the rest of them, the very problems that had brought them to CNC had yielded strengths that had helped them survive. Yes, Ian was a TV addict. But his Discovery Channel knowledge had saved their lives time and time again. The same was true of Charla's obsessed athleticism. Will and Lyssa had been shipped out because of an inability to get along. Yet hidden somewhere inside the fighting had been a loyalty to each other that grew stronger even as Will's health failed. And as for Luke, it was misplaced trust that had started him on this roller coaster. But that trusting way had made him the only one who could bring this rag-tag band of castaways together and keep them from losing hope.

That left just J.J. What was his special talent?

Spoiled brat, flake, impulsive hothead. Not exactly an impressive résumé.

How would *that* help the castaways through the most terrifying experience of their lives?

CHAPTER TEN
Day 23, 1:25 P.M.

Charla shinnied quickly up the narrow palm tree. Twenty feet below, Luke, Lyssa, and Ian craned their necks, regarding her nervously.

"Quit staring!" she called down in annoyance.

But they continued to follow her effortless progress up the trunk. Did they expect her to fall and kill herself? When were they ever going to figure out that this was easy for her? Compared with a back giant, long-hang kip dismount from the uneven bars, this was nothing!

She continued her climb up the smooth trunk. The tree was tall — fifty feet, she guessed. But she wasn't going all the way to the top. There she'd be lost in the canopy of the rain forest, out of touch with the ground. When she was about thirty feet up, she stopped and signaled the others.

It wasn't exactly a panoramic view — in heavy jungle there was far too much foliage in the way. But this was the closest thing to a lookout spot they were going to find on this side of the island. She couldn't see the Quonset hut, of course. The plant life around it was too dense. But she'd see the smugglers when they came to continue their search for the money. At least she hoped she would. Charla's signal would tell the others where to drop the suitcase. She had to pay careful attention. Their lives depended on it.

An hour earlier they had found the suitcase exactly where Luke and Charla had left it — on the edge of the small clearing.

"How could they miss it?" Luke had asked in disbelief.

From the clearing, it was the most obvious thing in the world. But Charla could see how, just a few short yards into the jungle, it disappeared in the thick weave of foliage.

The waiting began. Now *that* was every bit as hard as being a star athlete. Hanging in a tree was easy, but hanging there for *hours*, knowing that if you let your guard down . . .

No, don't think about that.

Hours. It felt more like months. Thirty feet below, she could see the others talking among themselves. The image made her feel alone and resentful. Stupid, she realized. Who else could do this?

It was amazing that, even after all these weeks, she was still so suspicious of the others. Were they talking about her behind her back?

About how she was the poor girl whose father worked three jobs to support her training, and who went into debt to pay for CNC?

She shook her head to clear it. Yeah, they knew. But why should they care? They had their own problems to worry about. If there was a bright side to their terrible predicament, this was it: Being shipwrecked was a great equalizer. According to J.J., his father made thirteen million dollars a movie — twenty working lifetimes for her dad. But here they were both castaways. And neither was better, richer, safer, or more comfortable than the other.

When she saw the movement, it took a moment to identify it. Tiny gaps in the leaves and tall grasses gave glimpses of colored shirts, almost like staccato pulses of light.

Deep shock. She wasn't surprised that the smugglers were coming, but by how *close* they were before she spotted them. She tried to give the signal — the hooting of an owl. But she was breathing too hard and couldn't seem to manufacture the sound. Thinking fast, she kicked off a tattered sneaker and watched it drop.

Coming from thirty feet up, when it hit Luke in the shoulder, the impact knocked him to his knees. By this time Charla was already scrambling down the trunk. She leaped the last five feet, stepping into her shoe.

"They're coming?" Luke whispered.

"They're *here*!" Charla hissed back.

Lyssa and Ian looked around desperately.

And then they heard the swishing sound of legs plodding through the vines and bush.

Luke mouthed the word: *Freeze*, but the command was unnecessary. Fear had turned the castaways to statues. There wasn't even time to duck down into the underbrush. The men were nearly upon them.

Charla's mind worked furiously. What should they do? Fight? Run? She looked to Luke but his face was all horror and indecision.

A blue-jean-clad leg burst out from a fern not four feet away. She felt a scream forming in her throat. She shut her eyes tightly and grimaced it down. When she opened them again, his face was right there. Through the gridlike leaves of the fern, she recognized his red hair. This man was a murderer. The castaways had seen him kill one of his own people in cold blood.

And now he had found them.

Or had he? Looking straight ahead, Red Hair stepped right past them and disappeared into the jungle. Charla let out a low whimper and nearly choked on it. The other man was only half a step behind him.

She watched his beady eyes dart around. Had he seen them?

No, he was looking down — for the suitcase. She held her breath as he passed by.

The castaways stood frozen, breathing silent relief into one another's faces.

Lyssa was the first to speak, her voice barely a whisper. "We are so lucky."

"I don't feel lucky," Luke grumbled. "Now that those guys are past us, we'll be chasing them around all day."

"Wait here!" Charla snatched up the suitcase and ran off after the smugglers.

It was impossible to sprint in the jungle; a high-stepping jog was the best she could do. A low vine tripped her up, but she was able to use the suitcase as a shield when she collided with a tree. *Careful*, she admonished, speeding up again. If she knocked herself unconscious out here, only the snakes would find her.

As she ran, she formulated her plan. It was a classic outflanking move — used by track stars to get the inside lane. Setting herself on a course parallel to the smugglers, she raced ahead until she was sure she had passed them. Then she made a right turn, stopping where she estimated their path would take them. Hidden in the underbrush, she waited, the suitcase in her trembling arms.

Good-bye, megabucks. I'll never see this much of you again.

A thin smile came to her lips. Her whole life, money had been a worry. Now she had her mitts on a boatload of the stuff — in the one place where money meant absolutely nothing!

I wouldn't take it anyway, she thought. *It's dirty money, earned with the blood of endangered elephants and tigers.*

Crackling in the underbrush. The smugglers were here already! Only — where were they? Frantically, she looked around for the warning signs — swaying fronds, snapping twigs, hints of color behind the foliage. Nothing, except —

There, fifteen feet to her left, a stand of ferns was rocking. She had guessed wrong. And now she'd have to start all over again.

I can't do this. A whole day of shadowing these killers, trying to predict where they'll be —

Acting on instinct, she picked up the suitcase and hurled it with all her might into the smugglers' path. While it was still in midair, she realized the mistake she had made. If the men saw it

ESCAPE

land, they would know someone had thrown it.

A body pushed through the fern. Oh, no! She was caught!

But wait! Red Hair was turned away, talking to his partner behind him.

The suitcase landed with a soft thud. Money spilled out.

See it! See it! See it!

But he didn't. Charla was thunderstruck. She wanted to scream: *There, you idiot! Right in front of your nose!*

The jungle hit you with such a vast array of *details*. With that overload of input, it was possible to miss anything.

Red Hair was walking again. In a second he'd be past it. Charla was in agony. They'd never get the suitcase any closer than this.

And then . . .

"Ow!"

He stubbed his toe on it, looked down, and found himself gazing into two million dollars.

"I got it! *I got it!*"

Charla held her own silent celebration alongside the smugglers' raucous one.

"Now we can get out of here!" Red Hair exclaimed.

Music to her ears. She followed the smugglers at a safe distance, keeping an eye out for any landmark that might point her in the direction of the lookout tree, where Luke, Lyssa, and Ian should be waiting.

Suddenly, there was a yelp, followed by the crashing sound of someone tumbling through the underbrush. Her stomach tightened. Her friends!

But then she heard Red Hair's voice. "Chelton! You okay?"

"I fell in a hole!" came the muffled reply. "A *big* one. And — hey, there's something down here!"

Charla came up a few yards behind Red Hair, who was on his hands and knees searching the jungle floor for the other man. A familiar notch was carved into a palm trunk close to where he knelt. A feeling of deep dread took hold in her gut.

The smugglers had found the bomb.

SEPTEMBER 3, 1945
1240 hours

Colonel Dupont stared at Junior, which had been dangling at the end of the defective crane for more than four hours.

"And that's the only way to move it?"

"Ninety-five hundred pounds, Colonel," replied Holliday.

Lieutenant Bosco, communications officer, ran up. "HQ says the nearest hydraulic is in Tinian. They can get it to us in three days."

"Three days!" The colonel regarded the flurry of activity on the runway. There was almost a carnival atmosphere as the men loaded up the plane, looking forward to reunions with wives and families.

If he gave the order to wait three more days, he'd have a revolution on his hands. . . .

ISLAND

CHAPTER ELEVEN
Day 23, 5:50 P.M.

The day had started out hopeful for J.J. Lane. It didn't stay that way.

His one-of-a-kind sunglasses remained focused on the cloudless sky, now dimming, awaiting the arrival of the plane that would not appear — Charting a New Course, come for Will and, with any luck, the rest of them.

That had been one flaw in his reasoning — that CNC might try to rescue Will, the sickest, but leave the others to serve out their "sentence" of maturing and learning teamwork and building character —

And whatever else those professional torturers think we have to do.

For that reason, he was sticking to Will like glue. It wasn't exactly hard to do. Will had barely moved all day. He was burning with fever, and J.J. had the feeling the kid wasn't all there. Oh, he knew when he was hungry, or when he had to set out into the jungle to go to the bathroom. But one time when J.J. was helping Will into the trees, the boy said, "Get out of here, Lyss! I'm going to the can!"

ESCAPE

J.J. was taken aback. "It's not Lyssa, it's J.J."

Will seemed indignant. "My leg hurts, but I'm not blind," he muttered.

"They're coming to get us today," J.J. reassured him. "Just hang in there and you'll be okay."

And what was the bleary reply? "I hope Dad takes the tunnel. There's traffic on the bridge."

Two months ago J.J. Lane had been riding down Sunset Boulevard in the passenger seat of Leonardo DiCaprio's Porsche. Now he was the bathroom monitor on Gilligan's Island.

Instantly, he felt guilty for the thought. None of this was Will's fault.

J.J. scanned the horizon. Where was CNC? What was taking so long?

The waiting was hard, but he passed the time by imagining the looks on the others' faces when they returned to the campsite to see a rescue plane. Especially Haggerty. Luke always acted like he had some special confirmation from God that whatever he did was exactly the right thing.

A juvenile delinquent from some rusty old mill town who thinks he's better than me! If CNC comes, I'm going to rub it in Haggerty's face all the way home.

If? No, he meant *when.* CNC was definitely coming. They'd be here soon. Only —

He checked Ian's *National Geographic Explorer* watch — how this cheap piece of junk still worked when J.J.'s Rolex had dropped dead was one of the great mysteries of the planet.

6:15. Soon it would be too dark to land.

Maybe they were coming tomorrow.

But Will's sick now! For all they know, we're getting ready to cut him open!

CNC were jerks, but they wouldn't let a bunch of kids operate on a real person. It wasn't just crazy — it was illegal. They could all go to jail for that, couldn't they?

It didn't make sense. The struggle to reason it out felt almost physical — like a wrestling match in J.J.'s head.

If they knew, then they'd come. Why aren't they here?

And finally — the answer . . .

Because they don't know.

J.J. squeezed his eyes shut as if he could stop his weeping by sealing it inside. But his tears were a flood he couldn't control any more than he could reverse the explosion of truth in his brain.

"Quit sniveling, Lyss," mumbled Will, half asleep on the raft.

The others had been right all along. Charting a New Course was over. It had gone up in a fireball and sunk to the bottom of the Pacific along with the *Phoenix* and its unfortunate captain. All this — the island, the smugglers, the bomb — was *real*!

No one was watching them. No one was protecting them. They were on their own.

"No," he breathed. Weeks of desperation and fear crystallized into a single moment of perfect horror. "No!"

"Shut up, Lyss. I didn't hit you that hard," murmured Will.

J.J.'s heart was pounding like a pile driver in his chest. He had to go somewhere, do something — to move, to act. Otherwise this terrible feeling would destroy him.

Voices! He jumped at the unexpected sounds. The others!

Lyssa took in the stricken look on J.J.'s face. "Is my brother okay?"

"He's fine," J.J. said absently. "You know — for him. How did it go with the suitcase?"

"Good news and bad news," groaned Luke. "We got the suitcase delivered. But in the process, the smugglers found the bomb."

"You're kidding!" J.J. exclaimed. "So — what does that mean?"

"It's impossible to tell," Ian reasoned. "We can't even be sure they know what it is."

"They'll figure it out," Charla said grimly. "We did."

Lyssa looked scared. "Men like that — they'll do anything for money. Can you imagine what an atomic bomb is worth?"

"We're not going to give those guys the chance to find out," Luke said definitely. "They've got their money. They'll be leaving tomorrow. Tonight's the night I stow away with the cargo."

There was a chilling moment that mingled sheer fright with the acceptance that this was their only path.

Charla spoke first. "I wish there was some other way."

"There isn't," said Luke bleakly. "We've had almost a month to think about getting off this rock. This is the best we can do."

"And we have to do it now if we're going to help Will," added Lyssa.

Ian nodded slowly. All eyes turned to J.J.

"I agree," said the actor's son.

Luke was surprised. "Really?" They had been expecting him to give them a hard time.

"But with one change of plan," J.J. went on. "Haggerty doesn't go. It should be me."

"You?" Luke laughed bitterly. "I thought you wanted to be here on the beach to meet the CNC rescue party."

"I was wrong about that," J.J. said seriously. "I'm not wrong about this."

Luke glared at him. "You idiot! This isn't like extreme snowboarding, where you brag to your Hollywood friends about all your bumps and bruises! It could be a suicide mission!"

"That's exactly why I have to go," J.J. argued. "Look — no offense — you're nobody. If they catch you in the cargo hold, they'll blow you away without thinking twice about it."

Luke was disgusted. "And they won't shoot you because your dad's famous?"

"Not famous," said J.J. "Rich! They won't kill me. They'll try to ransom me off to my old man." He flashed a crooked grin. "He might even pay too. He's got to be feeling pretty guilty about sending me on this trip."

"Listen to yourself!" Lyssa exclaimed. "Everything's a joke to you. How can we trust you to take it seriously?"

Luke was shocked. "Wait a minute — you're *considering* this?"

"J.J.'s right, you know," came Ian's thoughtful voice. "That *USA Today* the smugglers had — the article wasn't about us; it was mostly about Jonathan Lane's son."

"J.J.'s picture was in that paper," added

Charla. "If the smugglers catch him, there's a chance they might recognize him."

"What good is that if he doesn't get the job done?" Luke exploded. "This isn't about who's in better shape if he gets caught! This is about sneaking away and getting us rescued! This guy'll be on Space Mountain at Disneyland when he'll suddenly remember, 'Oops, I forgot to tell the rescuers about Luke, Charla, Lyssa, Will, and Ian.' "

J.J. bit back an angry retort. "Listen, I don't blame you if maybe you think I'm a bit of a flake — "

"A *bit* of a flake?" raved Luke. "If you look up 'flake' in the dictionary, there's a picture of your ugly face! Don't forget whose fault it was that the captain got killed!"

"And who was right there with me when it happened?" J.J. shot back.

"Someone had to stop you!" Luke raged.

"And you sure did a great job of it!"

There was a rustling sound and Will turned over on the raft. "We're not fighting, Mom," he mumbled. "Honest."

Luke folded his arms across his chest. "I'm not putting my life in your hands," he said in a lower tone.

ESCAPE

J.J. looked him squarely in the eye. "You think I like it that it has to be me? I've spent fourteen years doing things the easy way. That's my style — coasting. Nothing would thrill me more than hanging out here while *you* risk *your* neck. But this has to work, and I'm our best shot."

CHAPTER TWELVE
Day 24, 1:25 A.M.

The flashlight beam cast a dim glow over the lagoon where the two floatplanes were beached. The rear of the twin-engine craft bobbed in the shallow water. The other — with a single engine — sat heavy in the sand, fully loaded.

"That's the one," whispered J.J. "Fatso's plane."

Luke grimaced. Now that they were faced with it, the plan seemed totally insane.

The good-byes back at the camp had been shattering. Charla, Lyssa, and Ian had cried openly. Even Will, drifting in and out of delirium, had picked up on the mood of distress. It was clear that the castaways thought they were sending a friend to his death.

If it wasn't so awful, it would be interesting, Luke thought. Had the six gone to the same school, they probably wouldn't even have noticed one another. Will and Lyssa, the only two who had known each other before CNC, had been lifelong enemies. Yet the terrible and tragic events of the past weeks had bonded the group into a unit so close that to tear one away — even J.J. — left a painful, gaping wound.

ESCAPE

Luke and J.J. crept out of the brush and made their way furtively down the coral slope to the beach.

The cargo hold was in the underbelly of the single-engine plane. Luke lowered the hatch cover, and they shone the beam inside. There were three large wooden crates that the smugglers used to transport elephant tusks. Smaller squarer boxes contained rhino horns. There were also two refrigerated units whose humming batteries confirmed they were in operation. These held vital organs and other body parts harvested from endangered species.

J.J. opened one of the ivory crates. Inside, wrapped in soft blankets, were two tusks, each about six feet long.

"No room," Luke whispered.

They moved on to the second crate. The tusks were shorter but fatter, so it was also full. They turned to the third box. Inside were two four-foot tusks, one of them broken.

"It'll be tight," said Luke.

J.J. shrugged. "Good thing I've been on the banana diet for the past month." He swung a leg into the crate.

Luke put a hand on J.J.'s shoulder. "It's not too late, you know. I can still do this."

J.J. clambered inside and lay down flat. From

the pocket of his fatigues, he pulled out his sunglasses and popped them onto his nose. "How do I look?"

Any reply stuck fast in Luke's throat. The truth was that J.J. looked exactly like a dead body in a coffin. Finally, he managed, "You remember the location of the island, right? Our latitude and longitude?"

"Oh, sure," J.J. said, grinning. "First you go to Hawaii, then you hang a left — "

"J.J. — " Could this kid ever be serious, even in a moment like this?

"I remember," the actor's son insisted. "I'll be back soon, okay? Don't operate on Will."

Luke felt himself starting to lose it. "For God's sake, be careful. *Think* before you act. There are no do-overs now!"

J.J. nodded. "You'd better get going." He helped Luke maneuver the lid into place.

Luke secured the box. It was the hardest thing he'd ever done. "You can breathe, right?"

J.J.'s voice was muffled. "If you make it home and I don't, tell my dad I'm sorry I never grew up."

As Luke headed back into the jungle on shaky legs, he noted that the kid had it wrong. J.J. *had* grown up — more in the last few hours than in fourteen years.

ESCAPE

*   *   *

Both planes took off at six-thirty that morning. The twin-engine, carrying Red Hair and the money, turned east into the rising sun. The single engine, with Mr. Big, the cargo, and J.J., banked southwest toward Asia.

Crouched in a finger of jungle that extended out over the beach, a bleary-eyed Luke followed the progress of J.J.'s plane until it had disappeared into the distant haze.

"Good luck, J.J.," he whispered aloud.

At the castaways' camp, all activity ceased at the first sound of the propellers' buzz. The fire was smothered, the stills were kicked down and buried in sand, and the raft where Will lay was pushed under cover of the trees. All watched in silence as the aircraft carried their friend and their hopes far away.

"Lousy lawnmower," muttered Will. "Can't ever get any sleep around here."

Remarkably, J.J. slept away the hours before takeoff — concluding that he was either very cool or very tired. He was not cool, however, when the motor roared to life. He practically jumped out of his skin, smashing his head on the lid of the crate. The noise was unbelievable, and the vibration was making his bones come unglued. It was like front-row seats at a Metallica concert (courtesy of Dad) times a thousand.

He was aware of the bobbing of the craft as it moved out from the beach. Then a brief but powerful acceleration, and they were airborne.

It's really happening, he thought. The train had left the station, and it was too late to get off. He couldn't escape the impression that his life had changed so completely that he was now somebody he barely knew. It was terrifying, no doubt about it. But he also felt very alive and excited. Whatever happened, he was sure that it was better than rotting away on that island.

He eased open the lid of the crate and looked around. There were no windows, but some light was sneaking in through the door seal, making it possible to examine his surroundings. He squeezed himself out of the box, keeping low to avoid hitting his head. It was even louder out here, and he could see why. The front of the cargo hold opened into the engine housing. He tried to climb into it, but the heat of the roaring motor drove him back.

When they came to unload the cargo, he'd better not be here. . . .

ESCAPE

CHAPTER THIRTEEN
Day 24, 3:20 P.M.

J.J. had never been good with boredom. In his world, a whole lot of people and money had always been devoted to the entertainment of J.J. Lane. But even a week adrift on the lifeboat and almost a month stranded on the island hadn't prepared him for this plane trip.

It was long — hour after hour, cooped up in a cargo hold where he couldn't even stand. Not a window to look out of. And through it all, a teeth-rattling, never-ending roar that drowned out all thought.

Where were they going? Mars?

Wherever it is, let's just get there.

Then he felt it — the beginnings of descent. A wild panic knifed through him. They'd be on the ground soon. And then what?

The turmoil in his head threatened to tear him in two, a wrestling match between a craving for excitement and a dark voice repeating, *You could be dead soon.*

It was a smooth landing, but to J.J. it was jarring and unexpected. As they taxied, jouncing along a bumpy runway, he silently went over the

ISLAND

details of his plan. It would work. It had to. His life depended on it — his and the lives of Will and the others.

The plane came to a halt, and the engine shut down. The sudden absence of all that noise was like falling off the edge of the earth.

There were voices outside and the slamming of a door. The time was now.

Taking a deep breath, J.J. rolled over to the engine opening, clamped his hands on a metal bar, and hoisted himself inside. It was still painfully hot, but bearable now that the motor was off. His elbow brushed against the engine block, and a searing pain caused him to snatch his arm back. There, on the sleeve of his fatigues, was a small brown scorch mark.

The curse was halfway out of his mouth when he heard someone fumbling with the catch of the cargo bay. Scrambling with his heels, he backed into a corner and tried to be very, very small.

Light flooded the hold. One by one, the crates were hauled out by men speaking a language that could have been almost anything. Then a voice with an English accent: "Yeah, we had a spot of misery on that ruddy island. Don't even ask why. Got a mosquito bite for every minute I spent there."

J.J. huddled in the shadows, hardly daring to

ESCAPE

breathe. And then it was over. The plane was un-loaded; the voices grew more distant.

He felt a great surge of relief and triumph. He'd pulled it off! Now all he had to do was lie low until the men went home. Then he could sneak out and find the nearest policeman.

Suddenly, without warning, the engine roared to life again. A blast of heat hit J.J. in the face, and he lost his grip on the bar. He dropped like a stone to the floor of the empty cargo bay.

Frantically, he looked out the open hatch. The plane was swinging around to park inside a large aircraft hangar. It was like being on display on a rotating dessert rack at a diner. There was no place to hide.

The element of surprise was his only weapon. He had to make a break for it.

Crawling on all fours, he scrambled to the edge of the hold and prepared to jump.

Do it! he urged himself. *Don't wait till they see you!*

When he hit the floor of the hangar, he was already running. First he made for the cover of a pile of tires. But excited shouts told him he'd been spotted. He shifted direction for the hangar doors, yelling, "Cop! Cop!"

Heart sinking, he took in his surroundings. Dense jungle flanked the single runway. This was not a busy airport, but a private landing strip. Which meant there were no police around — only enemies. He was alone and badly outnumbered.

J.J. was fast, and the electricity of the moment made him even faster. He gave no thought to where he was or where he might go. All his concentration was on escape.

The jeep came out of nowhere, slicing across the doorway to cut off his exit. J.J. tried to put on the brakes, but he was running too hard. His knees hit metal, and he bounced back, looking around desperately for a clear field.

There! To the left!

But just as he sidestepped the jeep, a beefy arm grabbed him around the neck.

The race was over.

On the same day that J.J. left on the smugglers' plane, Will Greenfield failed to wake up.

Lyssa was frantic. She had spent the entire day trying to snap her brother out of his stupor. She used everything from bitter-melon tea dribbled between his lips to pots of seawater splashed in his face. She slapped, pinched, and shook him, but with no result.

"Is he in a coma?" she asked fearfully.

Ian just looked bewildered. He loosened the

bandage on Will's leg and lifted it. The wound was an angry red, with threatening lines of lighter red emanating from the center like a sunburst. The skin around it was hot to the touch.

"He needs a doctor," said Ian, stating a fact that everyone had known for some time.

There was almost a click as the castaways made the same connection: a doctor — rescue — J.J.

"J.J.'s got to be where he's going by now," decided Luke. "If Will's going to get his doctor, we'll know in the next couple of days."

"What if no one comes?" put in Charla.

Luke took a deep breath. "Well, then we'll know that J.J.'s — that he didn't make it."

"If that happens, we'll have to operate," said Ian. "It'll be Will's only chance."

Luke went gray in the face. "Before he left, J.J. made me promise we wouldn't do it."

"Let's pick a deadline," Lyssa said bravely. "If we don't hear anything by that time, we've got to figure that J.J.'s — not coming. And we do our best to get the bullet out."

"I wouldn't wait too long," Ian advised nervously.

Luke thought it over. "Let's give J.J. a few hours to escape and find help. Then they have to put together a rescue team and come back here to find us." He did a rapid calculation. "Not tomorrow, but the morning after that."

He looked around the circle of faces. Everybody nodded in agreement.

On his broken piece of raft, Will slumbered on.

CHAPTER FOURTEEN
Day 24, 5:50 P.M.

On the island of Taiwan, off mainland China, a small private airstrip was the final destination for the smugglers' cargo of illegal animal parts.

In an empty storeroom in back of the hangar, J.J. found himself in a rickety bridge chair, opposite none other than Mr. Big himself.

The fat man had neither the time nor the desire to be pleasant. "What were you doing on that island?"

"My boat sank," J.J. replied earnestly.

Mr. Big reached out and delivered an open-handed slap right across J.J.'s mouth. "The truth, right now."

"Honest!" exclaimed J.J., tasting blood from a cut lip. "I was shipwrecked! I only stowed away with you guys to get out of there."

English Accent stepped forward. "Boss, you don't think he could be off that kids' boat trip that went down?"

"That was a month ago," said the fat man in the soiled green suit. "There's no way any of those kids could have survived for so long."

ISLAND

"It's amazing what you can pick up from the Discovery Channel," said J.J.

Another slap. This one hurt.

"How can I make you believe me?" J.J. exclaimed. "We left Guam on the *Phoenix* on July eleventh! Captain Cascadden was the skipper, and the mate was a guy named Radford. The *Phoenix* sank. I was in the lifeboat for a week, and I've been eating bananas and fending off lizards ever since."

Mr. Big considered this. His piggy eyes got even smaller. "And your fellow survivors?"

J.J. shook his head. "I was the only one who made it. All the others went down with the ship."

The fat man nodded to English Accent. "Naslund."

Naslund grabbed J.J.'s arm, forced it behind his back, and yanked it high.

J.J. gasped. The pain was unbearable. He had taken his share of cuts and bruises in his life, but this was different. This pain was being applied by a professional, who knew exactly what to twist and how hard to twist it. It was cold and calculated, like a chess move.

"Come on, boy," Naslund urged. "I don't want to snap your arm. Just tell us who else is on the island."

J.J. fought to reason through the pain. It was something the castaways had never considered

ESCAPE

in coming up with this plan. They had always known J.J. would be at risk if he got caught, but this scenario had not occurred to them — that he might betray the others, and the smugglers would go back to the island and kill them all.

"I was alone!" J.J. grunted.

A quick twist, and the agony was double.

"You're breaking my arm!"

"Who was with you on the island?" insisted Mr. Big.

J.J. thought of the others. In that instant, he knew that his friends were worth a broken arm. "Nobody!" he gasped.

Another yank. The jolt cranked up the level of pain higher than he could have imagined. Black inkblots began to stain the edge of his vision. He was going to pass out.

And then it was over. Naslund released him and he dropped to the floor, sucking air.

He heard the squeak of a chair as Mr. Big stood up. "Clean up afterward," he instructed his employee.

"After *what*?" From the corner of his eye, J.J. saw Naslund pull a small handgun out of his belt. It was like living a scene straight out of one of his father's movies. It didn't seem real. But it was happening *right now*! This stupid boat trip was costing him his life! He was going to *die*!

Die. The word echoed in his head like the tolling of a bell. It was unthinkable! Bad things happened — bad luck — lousy days. But not *this*!

He was so shocked and panic-stricken that he almost forgot his trump card.

"Wait!" he screamed into the gun barrel. "You can't kill me! I'm worth money! *Big* money! My father is Jonathan Lane!"

The two smugglers exchanged a look.

"It could be true, boss," said Naslund. "The news said Lane's kid was on that boat."

The gun disappeared from J.J.'s line of vision. He allowed himself to breathe again.

That storeroom became J.J.'s prison cell, where he was held under constant watch. His guards were two Asian men who stayed with him in four-hour shifts. They didn't speak English, or perhaps they just had nothing to say to him, because he never got a word out of either of them. Privately, he nicknamed them "Mean" and "Meaner."

Mean was the thief. He patted J.J. down for valuables and seemed really annoyed when all he got was the designer sunglasses. Meaner was the music lover. He brought along a tinny portable radio, and spent his shifts leaning against the door, listening to a country-and-

ESCAPE

western station. In between songs by George
Strait and Shania Twain, an excited DJ emitted a
flood of what sounded like Chinese, addressing
his listeners as "pardner."

His meals were fast-food packs of odd-tasting
instant noodles that came with plastic chopsticks.
He had thrown up from his first helping. After the
island diet — mostly fruit and taro — the food
seemed so rich and heavy that it lay in his stomach like a shotput.

Mean and Meaner found nothing more hilari-
ous than watching him trying to shovel and slurp his
dinner. Finally, Naslund took pity on him and con-
ducted a crash course on eating with chopsticks.

J.J. was absurdly glad to see the Englishman.
The hours and hours of not knowing what was
going on were even harder than the number
Naslund had done on J.J.'s arm.

"Did you talk to my dad?" he asked anxiously. "He's going to pay, right?"

"Don't get your knickers in a twist," was the
reply. "We've got to prove you're alive first." He
slapped a copy of USA Today into J.J.'s hands.
"Hold this up. And watch the birdie." He raised a
Polaroid camera.

"What's the newspaper for?" asked J.J.

"Don't block the headline," ordered the smuggler. "You have to be able to tell it's today."

Click. A whirring noise produced the picture, which began to develop.

"You're going to *mail* it? I'll be stuck here forever!"

Naslund shook his head. "We've got a friend who's a whiz with computers. The way he e-mails, it's like it just pops out of thin air, totally untraceable."

"Dad'll pay up," J.J. mumbled, mostly to himself. "He has to. He won't let me die."

Naslund chuckled. "You're a valuable little piece of merchandise, you know that? You might even fetch a better price than that atom bomb."

"You'll never sell that bomb," J.J. blurted without thinking. "You couldn't get it off the island. It weighs a million tons!"

Naslund raised both bushy eyebrows. "So you know about that, do you? Not as sweet and innocent as you'd like us to believe."

J.J. reddened and said nothing.

"Funny thing about that bomb," the Englishman went on cheerfully. "It's not the shell that's valuable; it's what's inside. I don't know how to take that stuff out — but I'll bet we can find somebody who does."

By the time he strolled out of the storeroom, J.J. was almost happy to be left with the country music stylings of Meaner.

ESCAPE

CHAPTER FIFTEEN
Day 26, 6:40 A.M.

Luke stood at the water's edge watching the sky lighten as dawn broke. No plane, no boat, no helicopter — no J.J. Time had run out on the boy from California.

He felt a twinge of guilt for all the times he and J.J. had locked horns. True, the kid was a flake. But a lot of Luke's resentment had been envy. With Jonathan Lane's money and connections, Luke would have been acquitted with an apology, not shipped off on Charting a New Course.

He studied the sand at his feet. There was no reason to be jealous of J.J. now. The poor guy was probably dead.

A light touch on his elbow. Luke jumped.

Charla stood beside him, her eyes huge. "Ian's getting the stuff together."

Luke didn't move. "I can't shake the feeling that if I stand here longer, I'll think of something we missed — something that means we don't have to do this."

Soon the instruments were boiling in a pot,

ISLAND

and the bandages were rolled and ready.

Ian presented himself, paper-white. Lyssa was already crying silently. She sat cross-legged beside her unconscious brother, cradling his limp hand in both of hers. The beach was their operating theater; the sun provided their work light.

First came a shot of fifty-six-year-old Novocain. Even though Will was unconscious, Ian had heard that the trauma of the operation could jolt him awake. That was unthinkable.

They waited. Five minutes passed to allow the freezing to take effect.

"Will that stuff even work after so long?" asked Lyssa in a whisper.

Ian could not answer. It was just more evidence of how little they knew about what they were doing. In any other situation, they would be arrested and locked up for trying this on a living creature. How had things ever gotten to the point where this butchery was the only choice?

And then it was time.

Charla held out the tray of sterilized instruments. Ian reached for the scalpel, but couldn't make his fingers work. His hand started to shake, and when Luke looked at him, he realized that it was the younger boy's whole body that was trembling.

Gently, he moved Ian aside. "I'll do it."

When the sharp blade pierced the skin, Luke was amazed at how easy it was. It reminded him of slicing into an orange with an Exacto knife from art class. He looked anxiously at Will, expecting him to jump up screaming. But the patient slumbered on. He cut a neat slit about one inch long right through the center of the bullet hole. For a second he could see the thin red line. Then the blood oozed and spilled over.

He fought through a moment of light-headedness and scolded himself inwardly. What did he expect — chocolate milk? Of course there was blood.

Charla did her best to clean off the incision with a sterilized cloth ripped from fifty-six-year-old toweling.

Luke put the scalpel back on the tray and picked up a pair of surgical tweezers. Grimacing in deep concentration, he inserted the instrument into the slit and began to probe around for the bullet. More blood. And resistance too. Since the tweezers couldn't cut, moving it around was difficult.

Panic bubbled up inside Luke. This was crazy! He couldn't do this! They were nuts even to consider it! He pulled out the probe and dropped it onto the tray.

"It's no good," he managed to rasp. "I don't feel anything!"

"We can't stop now!" sobbed Lyssa.

"I'm hurting him!" Luke insisted hoarsely. "I don't know what I'm doing in there! I might as well be using a pickax!"

Ian spoke up in a shaky voice. "I saw a show once where the doctors made a second cut across the first one. Like an X."

And because Ian's TV knowledge had never failed them, Luke picked up the scalpel and tried again. There was a lot more blood this time, enough to scent the humid air. Charla gagged, but kept on mopping.

Luke felt the difference immediately. The second incision had opened the wound further, and the tweezers moved easily through the torn flesh. Then suddenly he felt it — something small and hard.

"It's here!" he breathed. He began to probe more delicately, attempting to maneuver the tweezers around the bullet. Sweat poured off his forehead, stinging his eyes. Time and time again he felt the tines close over the slug only to slide off its awkward shape. A terrible frustration gripped his gut, magnified by the knowledge that every minute this went on could be damaging Will even more.

He was wallowing in blood now. There was far too much for Charla to sponge away. But Luke didn't need to see. He had that bullet, knew exactly where it was.

A wave of nausea washed over him. *Don't stop,* he exhorted himself. *You just have to find the right angle! A little luck and a little wrist action and —*

"Gotcha!" The tweezers held the slug fast. Without even daring to breathe, he drew the bullet straight up and straight out. It was maddeningly slow, but he couldn't risk losing his grip. At long last, the tweezers came free. And there was the slug — ugly, misshapen, gory, but out.

Ian opened one of the old bottles from the dispensary and poured alcohol into the wound. Then another fifty-plus-year-old antiseptic — iodine — painted a bright orange spot on Will's thigh.

Luke's hands, surprisingly steady now, fit together the edges of the incisions and applied pressure. Last came a piece of modern medicine — an adhesive steri-patch from the first-aid kit off the lifeboat. It stuck like a second skin, holding the cut flesh together.

At last, Luke leaned back. They had done all they could do. The rest was up to Will.

It was only when Luke got to his feet that he noticed his jaw ached from clenching his teeth. His head was pounding. He took three shaky steps and passed out cold, face-first in the sand.

CHAPTER SIXTEEN
Day 27, 2:40 P.M.

J.J. sat on the floor of the storeroom, leaning on one knee. His thoughts were hundreds of miles away, back on the island. It was a dumb thing to do, but he found himself trying to conjure up a vision of the other five castaways, almost as if thinking hard would patch him into their frequency and give him an update. What were they doing? Was Will all right? What did they figure had happened to J.J.?

Well, that was an easy one, he reminded himself. He hadn't sent help, so they assumed he was dead. He and Haggerty had talked about that — rescue would come quickly or not at all.

Hang in there, he tried to urge the others over all that distance. *As soon as Dad coughs up the ransom, I'll send the cavalry for you.*

What a disaster this mission had turned out to be. In his mind he'd always pictured himself either free or dead. Not locked in a bare room for days, with worry and boredom intermingling in him to form a lethal cocktail of — what? He didn't know, but it was driving him crazy.

ISLAND

Especially with that never-ending sound track of twangy music!

He regarded Meaner, who was draped against the door, chain-smoking. "Could you please change the station?" he asked as politely as he could.

The guard looked back at him. His expression was so blank that J.J. couldn't tell if he'd even heard, let alone understood.

J.J. stood up. "The *radio.* How about some *different music?*" He pointed to the small portable and covered his ears.

He had Meaner's attention, but the guy still didn't get it.

"Here — I'll do it." J.J. took a step forward. It was a big mistake.

Meaner jumped up, pulled out his gun, and pointed it at J.J., screaming in Chinese.

J.J. raised his hands. "Hold on! Don't get excited! It's just the music, okay? The *music!*"

The door was flung open, and in burst Naslund. The Englishman yelled back in two languages until finally he began to laugh. He turned to J.J.

"Don't like the concert, eh? Can't say I blame you."

"I just wanted to change the station," J.J. mumbled resentfully.

"No time for that now," said Naslund briskly. He grabbed J.J. by the arm. "Let's have a little chat with your father."

J.J. brightened. "He's here? He paid?"

"On the phone," the smuggler amended. "He wants to hear his little boy's voice before he ponies up the cash."

J.J.'s face fell the distance between speaking to home and actually going there. "Okay, where's the phone?"

Naslund hustled him out into the hangar where a Mercedes stood waiting. "Your daddy's probably got half the FBI tracing this call. We're going to take a ride to a special phone."

They tied a burlap sack over J.J.'s head and pushed him to the floor in the back of the car.

J.J. guessed that it was mostly highway driving at first, but then the Mercedes entered what must have been a city. There were frequent stops, and he could make out horns and motorcycle engines all around.

He heard Mr. Big's voice: "There's a cop on horseback. Sit the kid up."

So the sack was ripped off his head, and he was plucked from the floor and squeezed onto the backseat between Naslund and Meaner. They were in the middle of a bustling Asian city — Hong Kong? Shanghai? Neon billboards with

Chinese characters flashed everywhere. Hundreds of motor scooters threaded through the crush of vehicles. Just ahead, a mounted policeman was directing traffic. No sooner had J.J.'s eyes locked on the cop than he felt the muzzle of a gun pressed against his side.

"Don't even think about it," whispered Naslund.

J.J. stared straight ahead, his blood chilled to freezing. They passed the officer close enough to reach out a hand and touch his boot.

As soon as the policeman was out of sight, on went the hood, and J.J. was back on the floor.

There were a lot of stairs — forty-two, J.J. counted. Every landing seemed to have a different cooking smell. Weeks on the island had gotten him used to the heat, but this was stifling.

When the burlap sack was finally pulled off, he was in a small seedy apartment crammed full of computer equipment and piles of books and manuals.

J.J. looked around for the phone, but Naslund sat him down in front of a computer that ran some kind of Internet long-distance calling program.

A young Chinese man with shoulder-length hair was expertly pounding the keyboard. He

ESCAPE

turned to Mr. Big. "It will be untraceable for two minutes."

They heard a single ring and a quick pickup. "Jonathan Lane."

It was all J.J. could do to keep from bursting into tears like a two-year-old. Since he'd last spoken to his father six weeks ago, the whole world had gone crazy. He'd been shipwrecked, marooned, and held at gunpoint. And here was this voice that came from a life before all that. It was a comfort and a torment at the same time.

"Hi, Dad."

"J.J., you're okay, right? They haven't hurt you?"

"I'm fine," he said shakily. "No, I'm not! You've got to get me out of this, Dad!"

"It's being taken care of," promised his father. "Just sit tight and stay calm."

"*Fast!*" J.J. insisted, agonized that he couldn't tell his father about the castaways still on the island. "You have to come quick! That's the most important thing!"

His father's voice was choked with emotion. "I know you're scared, J.J. But for me this is *happy!* Three days ago I thought you were dead! To talk to you, hear your voice — you can't know what it means to me — "

J.J. was struck dumb. His father was *crying!*

Jonathan Lane never cried, not even in the movies. He had instructed his agent never to consider a role that involved "blubbering."

Mr. Big grabbed the microphone. "This is all very touching, but we have business. I assume you've got the money?"

"It's ready."

"Good. You get your plane fueled and sitting on the tarmac, and when the time comes, we'll tell you where to fly." He made a cutting motion across his throat. The longhaired man broke the connection.

Naslund let J.J. sit up in the car and look around on the drive back to the hangar. He even provided a bit of a guided tour. This was Taipei; there was downtown; the Grand Palace was on that hill; the haze was air pollution.

Air pollution. Smog. J.J. never thought he'd miss it. But after six long weeks, this was his first faint echo of his beloved L.A. In spite of himself, he couldn't help but enjoy the action and feel of a busy, crowded city.

Idly, he wondered about the change of attitude among his captors. *They're in a good mood. They know they've got a big payday coming.*

It made sense. On the way over, they couldn't let him see his surroundings for fear that he might

ESCAPE

let slip something to his father. But now that the phone call was over . . .

He frowned. What was to stop him from giving up the smugglers once he was safe at home in California? He knew their location, their airstrip, and their secret island. He knew their faces and could testify against them and probably put them away for a thousand years.

How could they take that risk?

When the answer came to him, he realized that a part of him had always known it: He was never going to see California or his father again. When the smugglers had the ransom money in their hands, he was going to be killed.

CHAPTER SEVENTEEN
Day 28, 11:15 A.M.

Will Greenfield came awake into a world of pain and confusion. His leg was on fire.

What happened? Yeah, it hurt before, but not like this!

He sat up and practically passed out from the effort. Trickling moisture on his cheeks. He was *crying*! Sure, they'd all cried in the past few weeks — from terror, anger, hopelessness. Only a baby cried from pain. *But it hurts so much!*

He looked down. One entire leg of his fatigues was cut off, laying bare a thigh that looked like it had taken a direct hit from a cannonball. A square patch, crusty with dried blood, sat over the bullet wound at the center of a bright orange circle of iodine. Around that was an area of black-and-blue bruising that extended from knee to hip.

"Lyssa?" His voice was barely a rasp.

No answer.

"*Lyssa!*" He tried to drag himself to the flap of the sun canopy. Every inch of movement made his leg erupt with a searing agony. He had to bite on his sleeve to keep from screaming. *Come on,*

ESCAPE

you can do this. With a muffled moan, he crawled forward and peered outside. An amazing sight met his eyes. The beach was a beehive of activity. Nine stills worked side by side, boiling the salt out of seawater. Enormous stacks of fruit stood everywhere — coconuts, bananas, mangosteens, jackfruit, and durians, all waiting for — for what? The castaways could never eat that much stuff.

Speaking of eating, was he hungry? He thought so, but he could hardly feel his stomach over the explosion in his thigh.

Ian and Luke passed his line of vision, carrying something odd. It looked like a sort of blanket made out of army fatigues sewn together. And it was stretched between the two oars that came with the lifeboat.

How long have I been sleeping? What did I miss?

And then it hit him. That looked like — a *sail!*

"*Lyssa!* Lyss!"

This time the others came running. And when they found him awake and alert, the celebration was boisterous. He couldn't get a word in edgewise. When he opened his mouth to ask what was going on, Lyssa stuck a thermometer in it. That was when Luke explained that Will had been out for the better part of a week, and during that time, the bullet in his leg had been surgically removed.

"Without asking me?" blurted Will, spitting the thermometer clear out of the lifeboat.

Lyssa retrieved it and brushed the sand off. "And it worked, Will! Your temperature is almost down to normal! We thought we'd killed you for sure!"

"It feels like you did," Will gasped. "My leg, anyway. Why'd you have to do it?"

"This is better," Ian insisted. "I know it hurts, but that infection could have been fatal."

Will nodded slowly, struggling to think through the firestorm of pain.

"What's with the" — he strained to point at the beach — "the fruit market? And that thing between the oars?"

Luke took a deep breath. "J.J. stowed away on the smugglers' plane," he said gravely. "We haven't heard from him since."

It was the one thought that could have drawn Will's mind off his leg. "Oh, my God, they killed him!"

Luke nodded grimly. "We think so. And we also think they probably interrogated him before they did it."

"Which means they're going to come after us," Lyssa went on. "And this time there's no

ESCAPE

place to hide. We've got to get away from here."

"But not on the ocean!" Will protested, panting with the effort of his words. "Don't you remember? We almost died out there!"

"But this time we'll be prepared," Charla insisted. "We've got the lifeboat, and we're stocking up on food and water."

"Come on," groaned Will. "We'll never carry enough water to get us across the whole ocean!"

"No," agreed Ian. "But maybe the wind will take us into the shipping lanes or someplace where planes fly over, and we can be spotted. It's a long shot, but it could be our only chance."

"We can't just wait here to be slaughtered," added Lyssa.

Will lay back in torment and despair, staring up at the sun canopy. No, they shouldn't sit around waiting for their own murders. But was the only alternative to go out and quite probably kill themselves?

CHAPTER EIGHTEEN
Day 28, 11:45 A.M.

The country music was louder than ever, and Meaner was in an especially foul mood. That morning his fellow guard, Mean, had failed to show up for work, leaving Meaner with a triple shift as J.J.'s jailer.

The actor's son lay on his stomach on the hard concrete floor, his chin resting on folded arms. He had not set foot outside the storeroom since his guided tour of Taipei a day and a half before. He couldn't remember the last time he'd slept.

They're going to kill you. The thought was a heavy-duty wake-up call, a piercing alarm broadcast directly into his brain whenever drowsiness was about to get the better of him. If Dad paid up, the smugglers would shoot him the minute they had the money. But even if Dad held out, they'd eventually get wise and whack him anyway.

Better to stay awake, he told himself. *Don't sleep through any of the little time you've got left.*

Even after the shipwreck and all those terrible weeks on the island, this was the first time J.J.

ESCAPE

had thought seriously about what death would feel like. Blackness. Nothingness. But just for him. That part was especially hard to accept. The rest of the world would go about its business. In California, there would be traffic and surfing and all-night Hollywood parties. On the island, his fellow castaways would continue to think about rescue. Even this lousy music would probably go on.

"Howdy, pardners!" enthused the DJ. A string of lightning-quick Chinese was followed by the word *hoedown*.

My last memory is going to be Boxcar Willy.

He stood up. "I'm changing the station."

Meaner regarded him, a bored expression on his face.

J.J. headed for the radio. "I'm serious. There's got to be some decent music around here."

The guard barked something at him. His hand hovered over the gun in his belt.

J.J. swallowed hard and kept walking. A plan was taking shape in his mind.

He didn't shoot me last time. . . .

Now the gun was out. The man yelled a steady stream of agitated Chinese that mingled with the DJ's harangue to sound like a heated argument.

So long as he thinks I'm just a country music hater.

"Changing the station, got it? I'm changing the station." J.J. reached for the dial.

Shouting, Meaner took a menacing step forward, and J.J. picked up the radio and swung it with all his might.

Smack! The portable made contact with Meaner's hand. With a cry of pain, the guard dropped the gun, which skittered across the cement floor.

J.J. lunged for it. He knew speed was his only advantage in a fight with an adult. If Meaner ever got him in a wrestling match, he was doomed. His eyes were locked on the gun — only a few inches away! He reached for it, but Meaner hurled himself bodily into the way.

Wham! He hit the floor between J.J. and the weapon. There was a sick-sounding *crack* as the guard's head struck the concrete.

J.J. sprang to his feet, but Meaner was unmoving. A trickle of blood trailed out of his ear to the floor.

J.J. picked up the weapon and stuck it in the waistband of his fatigues. He was free. But how was he ever going to get out of the hangar?

He eased the door open about an inch and peered through the gap. The building was deserted.

I couldn't get this lucky.

ESCAPE

He looked from every angle. The plane was parked, and the big hangar door was closed. But there was no sign of his captors, and he could hear no voices. All was quiet.

He took three tentative steps and then broke into a run. Where was the control that opened the hangar door? It was probably pretty obvious, but in his excited state he couldn't locate it. Then he spotted a small emergency exit in the corner of the building. He sprinted for it.

Locked!

He fought with the knob, shaking with all his might. Cold panic. Anger too. He was so close! How could fate do this to him?

The gun. It came to him in a series of flashes from at least a dozen of his father's movies. The cop/detective/secret agent shoots the lock to make his escape. But that was the movies. Would it work in real life?

There's only one way to find out!

Hand shaking, he held the pistol about six inches from the doorknob and took careful aim. He had never fired a gun in his life. He was amazed at how hard it was to budge the trigger. But once it began to move, it was like a toboggan — accelerating, inevitable.

Three sounds came in such rapid succession

that J.J. heard them all at once: the crack of the gun, a violent screech of splintering metal, and a yowl of pain. The recoil took the pistol clear out of J.J.'s hand. It clattered to the floor five feet behind him. The ruined exit door swung slowly open to reveal Naslund and Mr. Big. The Englishman was doubled over, clutching his side where the bullet had struck him. His shirt was stained with blood.

"You!" exclaimed Mr. Big.

Naslund reached out menacingly, but J.J. exploded through the doorway past him, convinced to the core of his being that the prize of this footrace would be his very life. The Englishman pursued until the pain in his side became too great and he pulled up short.

"Get the car!" he croaked.

His words sent ice water coursing through J.J.'s veins. J.J. pounded down the runway, footfalls resounding in his head like the beating of his heart. *Fly!* he exhorted himself. It was a moment of such crystal-clear purpose it was almost exhilarating: Speed equals escape — that simple law governed his entire universe. If it weren't for the terror that held him in its grip, he might have been cheering himself on.

He wheeled off the runway onto a dirt road.

ESCAPE

All at once, his field of vision was filled with the front grille and headlights of a car — coming up *fast!*

There was no time to get out of the way. J.J. vaulted onto the hood and rolled. A split second before the windshield hurtled into him, he tumbled off the car, landing in a heap in light underbrush.

The squeal of tires. "Freeze! Hands on your head!"

J.J. didn't respond to the command. There were no moves left in him. Instead, he steeled himself for the impact of the bullets that would end this crazy ride.

"Geez, don't shoot!" shouted another voice. "It's him! It's Lane's kid!"

That was when J.J. took note of the vehicle that had almost obliterated him. It was a police cruiser.

CHAPTER NINETEEN
Day 28, 8:50 A.M.

"*Row!*" bellowed Luke.

He and Charla splashed through the waist-deep surf, pushing the loaded lifeboat out to sea. On board, Ian and Lyssa heaved at the oars, propelling the covered raft into the oncoming breakers.

The tide was going out, but the seas were rougher than usual. Every time they made any progress, a powerful wave would take hold of the craft and send it careening back toward the island.

Will's cries of pain resounded from the raft. With the wild pitching of the sea, it was impossible to keep his injured leg immobilized.

"We're hurting him!" shouted Lyssa, her voice barely audible over the pounding of the surf. "Let's try again when the ocean calms down!"

"No!" exclaimed Ian. "We make our move when we've got the tide!"

A breaker hit Luke in the face. He came up sputtering. He would have been overjoyed to postpone their departure until conditions were better. But the smugglers could already be on

ESCAPE

their way back to the island. Waiting an extra day might well be fatal.

"I hate this place!" raged Charla. "Getting here almost killed us and getting away is going to finish the job!"

Suddenly, the raft was in the grasp of a monster swell. For a breathless few seconds, it teetered on the crest, looming over Luke, threatening to come down and crush him. He was frozen, powerless to move, staring up at the terrified face of Will, who stared back at him through the flap of the sun canopy.

After all I've survived, Luke thought ruefully, *I'm going to be drowned by my own lifeboat!*

His eyes searched out the telltale foam that meant the wave was about to break. It never came. Instead, the raft bobbed up to the top of the swell and disappeared down the other side. The moving mountain of water rolled over Luke and Charla, driving them under.

Luke floundered, kicking for the light. When he surfaced, choking and spitting, he looked desperately around for the lifeboat.

Charla pointed. "Out there!"

Luke stared. In only a handful of seconds, the raft was forty feet away. Now free of the incoming surf, it was being pulled out to sea by a relentless undertow.

The rowers, Lyssa and Ian, were paddling like mad to slow things down. Their efforts had no effect at all on the drag of the ocean.

"Swim for it!" called Luke, launching himself through the waves.

Charla took off, cutting the water like a cabin cruiser. Her powerful arms churning, she passed Luke and bore down on the raft.

Still swimming, he saw her heave herself up over the side. It was only then that he realized how very far the boat still was, and how tired and heavy his arms and legs felt. An overwhelming isolation gripped him. If he couldn't reach the raft, he'd have to swim back to shore. Then he'd be marooned *alone*.

Never! he vowed to himself. *I won't go back there! If I can't reach the others, I'll drown right here and now!*

The thought was a booster rocket. His arms windmilled wildly; his legs manufactured the strength to kick on. He could barely hear the shouts of the others over the pounding of his own heart in his ears. He closed his eyes and swam blindly. If he looked and saw the lifeboat pulling away, it would mean there was no hope.

Splash!

Something hit the water inches from his face. He pulled up, and his arms smacked right into it

ESCAPE

— the raft's life preserver. He barely had the energy to clamp himself onto it.

Charla and Lyssa hauled on the rope, pulling him alongside the raft. Even hanging on to the edge of the sun canopy, he was too exhausted to climb onto the lifeboat. Instead, he allowed himself to be towed for twenty minutes before working up the strength to accept his friends' help and clamber aboard.

What came next had been carefully scripted. The paddles were tied into the oarlocks, pointing straight up. Between them was stretched the makeshift sail. Next, the flat wooden raft that had served as Will's hospital bed was maneuvered out the flap of the sun canopy and dropped over the side. It contained forty-six shelled coconuts, tied tightly in place under a blanket taken from the military base. It bobbed in tow behind the lifeboat.

Totally spent, Luke found an empty space and slumped back. Even with the coconut stash trailing behind, there was more food than people on the lifeboat. Wedged between the bunches of finger bananas and the sacks of roasted durian seeds, he fell into a deep sleep.

Six hours.
For the first time, the island was completely

out of sight. Once again the castaways found themselves at the mercy of the sea.

"Why didn't I remember how much I hate bobbing around the ocean?" mumbled Charla. "Maybe I would have had the brains to stay back on dry land and take my chances with the smugglers."

Luke regarded Lyssa. The girl had suffered from terrible seasickness while on the *Phoenix*. Now her face was a telltale shade of oatmeal.

"Hey," he said kindly. "No one's going to get on your case if you have to hang your head over the side."

"Just don't barf on the coconuts," Will added weakly.

She cast him a withering glare. "Big talk from the guy who bled on everybody here."

"Lyss — "

But his sister's queasiness bubbled up inside her. With a strangled gurgle, she headed for the flap. She threw the canopy wide, then dropped back among them with a scream of shock.

Luke grabbed her by the shoulders. "What? *What?*"

The raft lurched and dipped to one side. A moment later, the head and shoulders of a man in a short-sleeved hooded wet suit were thrust through the opening.

ESCAPE

The effect was so stupefying that the castaways were turned to stone.

Luke's gaping disbelief changed abruptly to terror as his mind made the jump from bewilderment to explanation. The smugglers had tracked them down! This frogman was here to kill them!

He grabbed wildly for a weapon and came up with a heavy bunch of finger bananas. He reared back to take a murderous swing.

"U.S. Marines!" barked a commanding voice from behind the goggles. "Drop those bananas!" He rumbled a laugh into the stunned silence. "I never thought I'd get a chance to say *that*."

He spoke into a tiny mouthpiece that stuck out of his rubberized helmet: "Swimmer to base. Got 'em."

From his belt he pulled a razor-sharp eight-inch hunting knife. With a powerful sweep, he slashed through the sun canopy from one side to the other. Blinding light streamed in as the cover fell away, exposing the lifeboat to brilliant blue sky.

A roar from above drew five sets of dazzled eyes. A massive helicopter was moving into position over them.

Charla was the first to speak. Her voice was so shrill and full of disbelief that it was almost unrecognizable: "We're — *rescued*?"

The instant the word was out of her mouth, she began to cry. Each in turn, Lyssa, Ian, Will, and Luke gave in to the juggernaut of emotion. Twenty-eight days marooned. A week adrift before that. Suffocated with danger and fear. Surrounded by death.

And now — just like that — it was all over. It seemed almost unreal.

The chopper lowered a cable to the swimmer.

"Take my brother first!" begged Lyssa. "And watch out for his bad leg!"

The marine fastened the straps around Will. The boy turned his tear-streaked face to his fellow castaways. "You did it, guys. You got me out."

Then he was gone, winched up to the helicopter, where waiting hands pulled him aboard.

Luke's mind was in a fog as he watched the others drawn up to safety. *I'm going home.* Tentatively, he turned the idea over. It had been so long that he didn't really think of home very much anymore. It was even hard to picture his room or his parents' faces.

"Okay, kid," said the swimmer. "Last customer."

Luke allowed himself to be strapped into the harness. It was almost too easy. A kind of cheating. Five weeks of terror and struggle, and then a helicopter comes along — a Get Out of Jail Free card. He felt a pang of grief. If only all of them could have been here to play it.

His ascent to the chopper was faster than he expected. Two marines dragged him aboard and ripped the harness from him. He looked around for the others, but saw only one face — a million-dollar smile behind custom-made designer sunglasses.

"I came back for you, Haggerty," said J.J. in an injured voice. "You weren't there."

Luke grabbed him by the collar. "The smugglers?"

"In jail," beamed the actor's son. "And they're already looking for Radford."

Luke shook his head in amazement. "I can't believe you did it."

"Well — I had a little help."

Luke frowned. "From who?"

In answer, J.J. pulled off his shades and waved them in Luke's face. The inscription on the earpiece flashed in the sun: JONATHAN LANE, THE TOAST OF LONDON — PS.

Luke was impatient. "Yeah, yeah. You've got great sunglasses. Come on, how did you get away from the smugglers?"

"The guy they had guarding me tried to sell my shades," J.J. explained, "and the pawnshop owner wanted proof that the inscription was legit.

He got in touch with my dad's office, and they called the FBI."

"But how did they know where to find you?"

"The cops squeezed it out of my guard." J.J. grinned. "It was the glasses, Haggerty. I told you they were special."

Luke stared at the one-of-a-kind shades. He had always hated them; they were the ultimate symbol of J.J.'s cocky, Hollywood attitude. Never could he have imagined that they would save all their lives.

The chopper crew hauled the swimmer in through the door and sealed the sliding hatch. The helicopter banked southwest, heading back to its base.

"Guam in forty minutes," the pilot called to the castaways.

"You mean we're not going to the island?" Luke asked anxiously.

The swimmer put a hand on his arm. "Whatever you left there, I'm sure your folks'll get you a new one."

"It's not what we left," insisted Luke. "It's what you left."

"Us?" The pilot turned around to regard him. "We weren't even there."

"Not now," Luke informed him. "In 1945 — you forgot your atomic bomb!"

ESCAPE

SEPTEMBER 3, 1945
1805 hours

The tropical sun set on an island of impatience. The transport plane was loaded. Airmen jammed their hands in their pockets and tried not to fidget. The war was over. They should have left hours ago. What was the holdup?

Still hanging from the broken crane, Junior, the third atomic bomb, had been opened like a five-ton cookie jar.

Sergeant Holliday and Corporal Connerly watched as the technician removed two pieces of radioactive uranium that provided Junior's nuclear fuel.

For the most destructive weapon humankind had ever devised, the trigger was astonishingly simple. At detonation, the smaller uranium slug would be fired into the larger bowl-shaped piece to set off a nuclear blast strong enough to destroy an entire city. It seemed scarcely more technical than starting a fire by rubbing two sticks together.

The uranium pieces were packed in separate lead-lined containers. Next, the detonator was removed — an ordinary gun barrel hooked up to an altimeter. The components were put in the back of a truck to be driven to the airstrip and loaded onto the plane.

Holliday stared as the technician stepped onto the flatbed of the truck to accompany the nuclear material.

"Wait a minute! Where are you going? What about the bomb?"

The man patted the lead-lined containers. "The real bomb's in here, Sarge. That" — he pointed to the shell of Junior — "is a very expensive paperweight." And the truck drove off.

Holliday was annoyed. "Well, what are we supposed to do with it?"

Connerly surveyed the small crowd of airmen that had gathered around the bomb pit. "Anybody got a piece of paper?"

ESCAPE

EPILOGUE

When the six young people entered the lab, they were dressed in identical air force coveralls. This seemed completely appropriate, because the military doctors had never before seen such a close-knit group.

They demanded adjoining hospital rooms, ate every single meal together, and stayed up until all hours of the night watching the Discovery Channel in the lounge. They could not seem to get enough of one another's company and conversation.

Later in the afternoon, they were scheduled to fly to Hawaii, where their parents would be waiting to welcome them back from the dead. But that morning, they were guests of the highest-ranking general on Guam. He had declared that these six, of all people, had the right to be present for this procedure.

The six took their front-row VIP seats. They seemed fit enough, although they were thin and very sunburned. One of them was on crutches. Their eyes were focused on the concrete floor where the atomic bomb lay, its long body extending three-quarters of the way across the lab.

ISLAND

The operation began. Physicists and technicians cut their way through black metal and removed a large piece of the rounded side. The chief scientist beckoned the six forward. They approached gingerly. This was, after all, an atomic bomb, the most awesome man-made force of all time. It had scared them when they'd first stumbled across it on their island; it scared them now.

The compartment was empty, except for one small item. It was a yellowed sheet of paper that had been torn from a loose-leaf notebook. On it, in faded ink, someone had written a single word:

KA-BOOM!

The flash of the reporter's camera captured the moment — six castaways seized by the kind of laughter that could only come from those who had not truly laughed for a very long time.

That picture made it to the front page of every newspaper in the world.

On September 12, 2001, Calvin Radford, former mate of the *Phoenix*, was arrested in a waterfront bar in Macao. He was charged with six counts of attempted murder.

* * *

ESCAPE

On October 23, 2001, the International Geographical Commission made an addition to their map of the Pacific, a tiny cay at latitude 17'31" North, longitude 157'42" East. They called it Junior Island.

On December 28, 2001, the six castaways held their first reunion at the Los Angeles home of movie star Jonathan Lane.

They did not go to the beach.